KITCHO

KODANSHA INTERNATIONAL
Tokyo • New York • London

KITCHO
Japan's Ultimate Dining Experience

KUNIO TOKUOKA
CHEF

TEXT BY Nobuko Sugimoto

PHOTOGRAPHY BY Kenji Miura

TRANSLATED BY Juliet Winters Carpenter

CONTENTS

SPRING KAISEKI 12

SUMMER KAISEKI 48

Note: Japanese names are in the Western order, first name followed by family name, but in the traditional order for historical figures.

Distributed in the United States by Kodansha America LLC, and in the United Kingdom and continental Europe by Kodansha Europe Ltd.

Published by Kodansha International Ltd., 17-14 Otowa 1-chome, Bunkyo-ku, Tokyo 112-8652.

Text copyright © 2010 Kunio Tokuoka and Nobuko Sugimoto. Photography copyright © 2010 Kenji Miura. Translation copyright © 2010 Juliet Winters Carpenter.

All rights reserved. Printed in Japan.
ISBN 978—4—7700—3122—8

First edition, 2010
18 17 16 15 14 13 12 11 10   10 9 8 7 6 5 4 3 2 1

Library of Congress Cataloging-in-Publication Data

Tokuoka, Kunio
  Kitcho : Japan's ultimate dining experience / Kunio Tokuoka ; photography by Kenji Miura ; text by Nobuko Sugimoto ; translated by Juliet Winters Carpenter. -- 1st ed.
    p. cm.
  Includes bibliographical references and index.
  ISBN 978-4-7700-3122-8
  1. Cookery, Japanese. 2. Kitcho (Restaurant) I. Sugimoto, Nobuko, 1943-
II. Title.
  TX724.5.J3T6425 2010
  641.5952--dc22

                    2010015444

www.kodansha-intl.com

FOREWORD

I fell in love with Japanese cuisine when I first moved to New York in the 1980s as a young cook. I was struck by the clarity and simplicity of flavors, how the quality of each ingredient was paramount, and by the absolute reverence that its chefs displayed. I was especially intrigued by the art of kaiseki, long considered to be the haute cuisine of Japanese gastronomy. While I have only recently had the good fortune to travel to Japan and experience a traditional kaiseki meal, it was well worth the wait. It was one of the most profound experiences of my life and certainly one of the most memorable. Therefore, it comes as a wonderful honor to have been asked by Kunio Tokuoka, chef of Kitcho, the venerated Kyoto restaurant steeped in this tradition, to write the foreword for his upcoming book.

For a customary kaiseki meal, the journey is part of the anticipation. It is effortless to relax, as the amount of food you are consuming is the amount of food your body can absorb. It is an almost spiritual experience as you become attuned to everything around you, including the timing of the meal. What continue to strike me to this day are the extraordinary quality of the food and the richness of history expressed in every detail—from the antique cauldrons used to make tea for the Zen-like ceremony, to the gracefulness of the hosts and the serene backdrop of the surrounding mountainside. While everything about the meal is a direct reflection of this environment, it is the sense of "honoring the past" that makes you focus on the present—where you are, who you are with, and the emotions evoked at that particular moment.

Many of the guests who come to dine at The French Laundry liken the dining experience to a kaiseki meal: many small courses served in succession. My philosophy, while aligned with the traditions of this revered cuisine, was actually born from the Law of Diminishing Returns, and its provenance stemmed from more humble beginnings. Our philosophies may have different origins, but there are certainly unifying similarities.

It was early in my career as a chef, when I was at the beach on a hot summer day and was reaching for a bottle of beer, that I became aware of how much I anticipated having my first sip. It was everything I had hoped for. It was delicious and refreshing; it quenched my thirst and provided relief after many hours in the sun. My second and third sips, while pleasurable, provided nowhere near the satisfaction that I felt in the beginning, which further lessened as I drank the rest of my beer. It was then I realized that too much of the same thing eventually leads to palate fatigue. It was this viewpoint that ultimately translated into my cuisine, and I conceived of offering smaller dishes showcasing diverse layers of flavor in order to maintain a level of excitement and provide elements of surprise throughout the entire dining experience.

Another similarity that I believe we share is inspiration. People have often asked me what inspires me and I respond that it is easy to pinpoint what has done so in the past, but I do not know what will inspire me in the future. The key is awareness. One needs to be conscious of one's surroundings in order to see inspiration and be open to it. The menus at our restaurants are driven by the seasons and what is available in the market. The cuisine and environs at Kitcho reflect the same philosophy. The meals the chef and his staff craft each day show appreciation and harmony with their natural surroundings, as well as a willingness to embrace change by introducing touches of modernity—just as we all invariably evolve through the passage of time.

Chef Tokuoka's book *Kitcho* is in and of itself an inspiration. It gives us a wider glimpse of the beauty that he brings to the table; his expression of the world around him is demonstrated through the medium of food. While it might not be possible to completely re-create these very same dishes in our own homes, his work provides us with an opportunity to rejuvenate our minds, and allows us a moment of pause in order to be able to look about us with fresh eyes, focus, and clarity.

Thomas Keller
The French Laundry
Yountville, California

INTRODUCTION

Kitcho was the most famous restaurant in the Kansai region, perhaps in all of Japan. It was also frighteningly expensive, for it preserved the full traditions of personal service, private eating rooms, and seasonal dishes with only the highest quality ingredients. Every course was a delight to the eye as well as to the palate.

The restaurant described in this excerpt from *The Garden of Rama* by Arthur C. Clarke, one of the premier science fiction writers of the twentieth century, and his co-writer Gentry Lee, appears to be Kitcho, in the Arashiyama district of Kyoto. The novel came out in 1991 as a third sequel to *Rendezvous with Rama*, winner of the 1973 British Science Fiction Association Award. In it, a father and son discuss a trip to Mars over dinner. The scene that unfolds is memorable for its combination of futuristic theme and traditional setting. In real life, Kitcho remains exactly as described in the quote above, continuing into the twenty-first century.

Kitcho's founder, Teiichi Yuki, established traditions of cuisine and décor that were influenced by the tea ceremony. These were faithfully carried on by his son-in-law, Koji Tokuoka, who passed them on in turn to his son, Kunio. Today, firmly grounded in centuries of tradition—including the accomplishments of his father and grandfather—Kunio Tokuoka adds his own culinary techniques and insights to the world of Japanese haute cuisine, for the greater delectation of guests who flock to Kitcho from every part of Japan and overseas.

Kunio's unflagging efforts were rewarded in 2009 with a coveted three-star ranking in Michelin's first guide to fine dining in Kyoto and Osaka. Of course, the award was a tribute not only to the extraordinary quality of Kitcho food and service, but also to the restaurant's tasteful décor: the venerable calligraphy and picture scrolls, the impeccable flower arrangements and art objects, the delicate scent of incense, bowls of whisked green tea, and so on. In its carefully chosen decorations and unsurpassed hospitality and service, Kitcho maintains proud traditions of beauty and excellence. Though elsewhere they may be disappearing, at Kitcho these elements of high-end culture are safeguarded and daily renewed.

■ ■ ■

Kitcho's history began in 1930, in Osaka. Teiichi and his wife opened their first restaurant, Ontaicha-dokoro Kitcho (loosely, "Sea Bream and Tea Kitcho"), when he was twenty-nine. It was a hole in the wall with barely room inside for ten customers. Having learned to cook from his father, who was also a chef and the owner of a large restaurant, Teiichi decided to strike out on his own as he puzzled out an answer to the question "What is cuisine?"

What had set Teiichi to mulling this issue was encountering, at age twenty-four, records of tea gatherings held by Lord Matsudaira Fumai (1751–1818), the ruler of the Matsue domain (today's Shimane Prefecture) and a famous tea master. In studying menus from those long-ago occasions, Teiichi was struck by the deep sensitivity to the seasons that infused them. Inspired, he decided to open a new kind of restaurant, one that would offer a blend of such tea-ceremony cuisine and the way of cooking he had learned growing up. The essence of Teiichi's unique culinary style (which in later years he summed

up in a line of poetry as "Flowers, birds, wind, and moon: all nature is cuisine"), and of his gracious hospitality, was rooted in this youthful encounter with tea ceremonies of the past.

The clientele of the little restaurant in Osaka soon grew to include local business titans and devotees of tea. In Teiichi's choice of food and utensils, and in the ambience of the tiny but exquisitely appointed room, they discerned a rare talent. As his ties with these patrons deepened, Teiichi, too, entered the world of tea, eventually becoming a widely respected tea connoisseur in his own right.

This first Kitcho grew steadily in size and reputation, but there were also setbacks: in 1943, the restaurant burned to the ground in an air raid. After the war, Teiichi opened two full-fledged new restaurants, one in Kyoto's Arashiyama district and the other in Osaka. Though surrounded by well-known establishments with lineages going back two or three centuries, Teiichi quickly earned high praise for his devotion to the art of cuisine. Before long, he was being entrusted with meals for visiting nobility and Tokyo summit participants.

One of the happiest events in Teiichi's life occurred in 1981, when he became the first person in the culinary arts to receive the Medal of Honor with Purple Ribbon from the Japanese government. Then in 1988 he was awarded the Prize for Distinguished Cultural Merit—another first for a chef. At the time of the first award, he commented, "I'm extremely grateful that the government has recognized the importance of cuisine in my lifetime. I can only hope that this award may provide a stimulus for people in Japan to raise our native cuisine to the level of a high art, as the French have done with theirs, so that the glories of Japanese cooking may be known throughout the world."

A turning point for Kitcho came in 1991, the year Teiichi turned ninety. Until then, he had managed his fleet of restaurants himself, aided by his son and daughter-in-law as well as his four daughters and their husbands, but from that time on the several restaurants functioned independently. Besides the flagship restaurant in Osaka, there were now also Kobe Kitcho, Semba Kitcho, Tokyo Kitcho, and Kyoto Kitcho in Arashiyama, all entities unto themselves in cooking and management styles.

■ ■ ■

Next, let's examine the origins of the tea ceremony, which had such a profound influence on Teiichi and which continues to influence his grandson, Kunio, as well. The tea ceremony (called *chanoyu* in Japanese) involves inviting guests and serving them bowls of tea made by whisking powdered green tea (*matcha*) with water heated over charcoal or a charcoal brazier. Its modern form was established in the latter half of the sixteenth century as the Way of Tea (*sado*) by Japan's greatest tea master, Sen no Rikyu (1522–91). Rikyu's unerring taste had a profound impact on practitioners of tea. Moreover, he taught that in the tearoom, all are equal, and he emphasized the importance for the host of the precept *ichigo ichi-e*, meaning that every tea gathering is a unique, once-in-a-lifetime experience.

To heighten guests' enjoyment of the tea, the host may offer sake and side dishes or a light meal before the tea. It's vital, however, that the focus not be on gastronomical pleasures per se but rather on the significance of the occasion as people gather to enjoy an ineffable experience in one another's company. For this to happen, the host must oversee all manner of details—everything from the appearance of the garden to the choice of scroll painting and flower for the alcove, not to mention the various implements and utensils for preparing and serving the tea. Guests for their part appreciatively savor the unstinting lengths to which their host has gone to make the occasion memorable. This boundless mutual appreciation is precisely what makes for a once-in-a-lifetime experience. The sequence of events in tea may even be seen as a forum for spiritual training.

■ ■ ■

Historically, Japanese cuisine has been dominated by three main traditions: *honzen ryori*, still seen at banquets, wedding feasts, and the like; *cha ryori*, served with formal tea; and *kakeai ryori*, a more casual style where the food is cooked and passed over the counter to the diner, as tempura and sushi were at their inception. Of these, the second, though long held in slight regard, eventually became the dominant influence on formal dining in Japan—due in large part to Teiichi's contribution.

Honzen ryori is a highly formalized style of full-course cooking that arose in the Muromachi period (1333–1568) along with samurai etiquette. Each diner is served on low four-legged tray-tables called *zen*. The basic meal consists of one to three trays, but depending on the occasion there may be as many as seven, with perhaps three different kinds of soup and a dozen side dishes. Food for court nobles, meanwhile, in an ancient style of cooking known as *yusoku ryori*, featured a grand array of more than thirty different dishes per person served all at once. Teiichi wrote that the diner needed to consume only those that he or she fancied; the rest were a literal "feast for the eye."

Tea cuisine refers, as the name implies, to a meal served at a tea ceremony. It is also known as *kaiseki*, written with Chinese characters for "breast stone"; this word comes from the traditional practice among Zen monks of staving off hunger and cold during long bouts of winter meditation by slipping a heated stone inside their clothing. "Kaiseki" came by extension to mean a light meal, just enough to warm the stomach, and then, by association with the simple ideals of the world of *chanoyu*, the food accompanying a tea ceremony.

Teiichi defined the spirit of tea cuisine this way: "Taking every care to entertain guests by selecting seasonal foods at their peak and offering a meal of fine flavor, in moderation, with dignity and grace and in proper order." Part of the reason for emphasizing moderation is to ensure full appreciation of the green tea with which the meal ends. A typical kaiseki meal begins with an appetizer course (*mukozuke*) of sashimi or vinegared raw fish (*namasu*), followed by soup, a simmered dish, a grilled dish, a tray of *hassun* delicacies, an extra course of side dishes to accompany further rounds of sake (*shiizakana*), and pickles or *konomono*.

Kitcho's culinary style can be described as a cross between *honzen ryori* and kaiseki (for a typical kaiseki lunch, see pages 158–159). The latter, since it was relegated to the tea ceremony, was for a long time a mere side note in Japanese cookery. According to renowned historian Isao Kumakura, it was Teiichi Yuki's revolutionary vision that brought kaiseki into the limelight. Introducing a style of cuisine overflowing with a sense of the seasons may have been revolutionary in 1930s Japan but today, thanks to Teiichi, kaiseki is firmly in the mainstream of Japanese haute cuisine.

The seasonal sensitivity at the heart of *chanoyu* isn't about mere recognition of the shifting seasons; its true significance lies in its role as culture. The flowers, picture scrolls, tea bowls, and other accoutrements of the tea ceremony reflect seasonal change in prescribed ways, and so elevate this natural phenomenon to the level of a national culture. Teiichi's special genius lay in his intuitive response to the delicate seasonal spirit of the tea ceremony, and in his protean application and extension of that spirit through his métier, the art of cooking. In his lifetime he raised cuisine to the level of fine art—an art that reached its apex at Kitcho.

Clearly, Teiichi's successors at the legendary restaurant have much to live up to. Despite the daunting challenge of following in his father-in-law's footsteps, never mind overtaking him, Koji managed to faithfully preserve and extend the Kitcho style that Teiichi made famous. Now Kunio, the third-generation owner, has taken Kitcho to yet a higher level. Changing times affect people's preferences, as well as the speed of cultural transmission and a host of other factors that influence cuisine. "We at Kitcho can't go on making the same dishes that Teiichi did, in the same way, forever," says Kunio. "Our job is to pass on his ideals in ways suited to our time." This is the passion that keeps Kunio Tokuoka focused on continuing, through endless trial and error, the culinary revolution that his grandfather Teiichi began.

SPRING KAISEKI

A JAPANESE WORLD OF CUISINE À LA RIMPA

"It has always been my desire," says Kunio Tokuoka, "to create a Rimpa-style cuisine for the world to see."

"Rimpa" is a general term referring to a flamboyant yet elegant style of Japanese painting associated with a series of renowned painters and craftsmen, including Hon'ami Koetsu, Tawaraya Sotatsu, Sakai Hoitsu (pages 36–37, 75, 114, 157) and the shining stars of the style, the Ogata brothers, Korin and Kenzan (pages 46–47). Running off and on from the seventeenth to nineteenth centuries, it is a style that is at once fresh, invigorating, and inspirational.

In its day, the Rimpa style was a disrupter, a new and vigorous movement that challenged the accepted schools of painting whose roots stretched back centuries. Rimpa became popular among the common people, those outside the ruling aristocracy and warrior classes. At the beginning of the seventeenth century, this meant the rising merchant class: working people who established their own trade or business and prospered, or at least were able to better their position in life. While the aristocrats of the imperial court and the upper-class samurai of the shogunate authority mostly remained attached to the classic modes of painting, the vigorous activity that the era's peace birthed gave rise to an energetic new art form that reflected the spirit of the day. To many people, that spirit looks just as fresh—and just as inviting—today.

On the facing page is a gilded serving boat fashioned from the thin outer husk of a bamboo shoot. Kunio's grandfather, Teiichi, began making these after hearing about an episode in which the artist Korin, invited to a cherry-blossom-viewing party, brought food wrapped in a husk decorated with raised gold lacquer, in a playful expansion of a then-popular wrapping style. Although it is not known exactly what kinds of food Korin brought, Teiichi chose to array a tempting selection of delicacies in his boat-shaped husks: three slender skewers holding bite-size morsels of simmered bamboo, river trout grilled with white sake, cooked prawns, tubular steamed fish cake, crisp Japanese cucumbers, and more mouthwatering tidbits that remain a memorable combination to this day.

For the spring offering shown here, Kunio selected *Pan-Roasted Rice Balls—*

Pan-Roasted Rice Balls. Set in gilded bamboo husks, these tasty mouthfuls are topped with toasted rice after being carefully pan-roasted. See Food Notes at the back for details.

a seemingly simple food far removed from haute cuisine. Yet in this modest offering, he manages to combine three distinct taste sensations in each bite by a virtuoso blending of steamed rice, seasoned flavoring agents, pan-roasting, and textural accents. Needless to say, rice balls as delicate and tasty as these are a rarity. Nearly three centuries after Korin's passing, Kunio arranges his humble-seeming rice balls on a gold bamboo husk in his own distinct Rimpa style, at once carrying on and expanding tradition.

SERVING VESSELS AT KITCHO

There are many aspects to the pleasure of dining at Kitcho: the taste, selection, and presentation of the food; the rooms that evoke a subtle elegance; the sense of beauty in harmony with the seasons; and the gracious hospitality of the kimono-clad *okami*, or proprietress, and her entire staff. Also indispensible is the parade of decorative serving vessels, many of them art pieces—whether modest or grand—and the visual show they offer when matched with each course. The art of combining the perfect vessel with the perfect food adds yet another layer to the kaiseki experience, making dining at Kitcho that much more memorable, the sensory experience of a lifetime.

PREVIOUS PAGE: A detail from a Rimpa-influenced screen is placed in Kitcho's "Azumaya" room in the springtime. It takes as its motif the red-and-white command-post curtain also said to have been used by the great medieval military leader Toyotomi Hideyoshi at his famous Daigo cherry-blossom-viewing party of 1598. Magnificently adorned with paulownia crests.

THIS PAGE: Teiichi commissioned the diminutive covered dishes at right for his restaurant; his inspiration was a poem by Ariwara no Narihira (portrait below left) that refers to "Miyako birds" as a reminder of his beloved Kyoto. The portrait is an Important Cultural Property dating back to the thirteenth century.

Kaiseki can be served in a variety of ways. A ten-course meal, for example, would be served in ten or more vessels of different materials, shapes, and colors. Since dishware is chosen with careful reference to the season, month, festivity, and other aspects of the occasion, a kaiseki establishment must stock a vast assortment. When asked how much "tableware" has accumulated over the years, Kunio gives a shrug and a wry smile. "Don't ask me. All I know is, we have a whole lot of it."

Certain foods are invariably served on one piece and no other. By long tradition at Kitcho, the *Marbled Sole Sashimi* pictured on page 56, for example, is always arranged on an antique blue-and-white porcelain platter so that the underlying design can be enjoyed through the translucent, paper-thin slices. The elegance of the four-hundred-year-old platter is exquisitely set off by the luscious slices of raw fish, imparting an atmosphere of luxury.

The cupboards of Kitcho are filled with so many different pieces of serving ware, gathered with a practiced eye over the years, that Kunio must refer to a

Wild Greens and Red Ark Clam with a Tosa Vinegar Gelée. Lifting the lid of a bird-shaped dish reveals tender strips of boiled red ark clam and lightly cooked seasonal wild vegetables.

The rustic "Azumaya" room, one of Kitcho's dining areas, in spring. The room boasts a classic Japanese display alcove for art—perhaps a hanging scroll—and a flower arrangement, as well as sliding panels that can be pushed aside for a view of the garden if the weather permits.

master list in order to locate the one he has in mind. At other times, he uses the list to dig up seldom-used or forgotten pieces, or to search for an appropriate vessel for a new food creation.

"Serving vessels," rather than "tableware," is a more accurate term in talking about the range of "dishware" at Kitcho. There are truly all kinds, including everything from porcelain and earthenware to glass, lacquerware, shells, and, as seen earlier, bamboo husks. Some items have a long history, others are the creation of artists of Teiichi's, Koji's, or Kunio's acquaintance, and still others are original works that one of the three commissioned, sometimes inspired by an historical event or literary classic.

■ ■ ■

The serving vessels in the spring section represent a notable sampling of Japanese dishware. First is a work by the artist-potter and restaurateur Rosanjin Kitaoji, who famously said that "Dishes are clothing for food." Rosanjin was a twentieth-century potter who, after making a name for himself as a calligrapher and seal carver, approached the culinary world with vigor and devoted himself to making serving dishes that he would enjoy eating from himself. Today, his highly prized works continue to offer inspiration for newer generations of potters and artists, as well as raising the bar for what quality restaurateurs should stock.

The artist-potter knew Teiichi well. "Rosanjin used to come by often to see my grandfather, and would usually stay for dinner," says Kunio. "When he dined officially at the restaurant, he never paid in money but in work, which he would send later in batches. We treasure and use his works to this day." Kunio selected Rosanjin's rectangular Bizen stoneware dish (right) to serve *Assorted Sashimi in Flowing Water* and the decorated bowl on page 39 for *Bamboo Shoot Mélange*.

Teiichi was well versed in classical tales and ancient customs. As mentioned earlier, the gilded bamboo husk pictured on page 15 is based on an episode involving Ogata Korin. Teiichi recounted the event in his book *Tales of Kitcho Flavor*. One spring day, Korin joined feudal lords and noblemen for a blossom-viewing picnic in the outlying area of Kyoto known as Arashiyama. While the others brought elaborate boxed lunches carried by attendants, Korin produced only a small bundle wrapped in a bamboo husk. The party ate aboard a boat on the river for blossom-viewing, and after the meal Korin threw his wrapper into the water. As it drifted away through a flurry of cherry petals, all were amazed to see that inside it was painted with raised gold lacquer. Korin's "serving vessel" had began life as part of a plant, was next used to wrap food for a day on the river,

Assorted Sashimi in Flowing Water. An artful arrangement of extra-fatty bluefin tuna, red sea bream, and squid sashimi on an imposing stoneware platter by renowned artist-restaurateur Rosanjin. Details on the sashimi can be found in the Food Notes.

Clear Chicken Kelp Soup. This play on a traditional Japanese clear soup combines kelp stock with chicken wings and bones for a rich yet subtle broth. Aroma and taste are heightened with a garnish of long onion and tender leaves of Japanese prickly ash.

Venus Clam Soup. This delicate, multi-flavored soup features kelp-and-clam stock with clams and tofu, topped with a trio of fragrant garnishes.

and ended its service as a floating surprise. Based on that story, Teiichi had a lacquer craftsman coat a set of boat-shaped bamboo husks with gold lacquer.

Teiichi, Koji, and Kunio have derived their inspiration from many sources. For the small bird-shaped dishes on pages 16 and 17, Teiichi's creative spark was lit when he obtained a framed portrait of the ninth-century *waka* poet Ariwara no Narihira from the thirteenth-century "Picture Scroll of the Thirty-Six Poetic Geniuses." Teiichi had a ceramicist friend make a set of lidded dishes in the shape of birds in reference to Narihira's most celebrated poem, which was written in nostalgia and loneliness when the poet was far away from his home in Kyoto. The poem was inspired, the story goes, when Narihira asked the ferryman the name of the birds on the River Sumida and received the response "Miyako birds" ("Miyako" being an alternate name for the then-capital of Kyoto): "If you are true to your name / then let me ask you / oh capital-bird / Does the one I love / still wait for me?"

In Japan, high-end serving pieces often carry their history with them, and the pedigrees are not only interesting to trace but also become another point of enjoyment when the vessels are next used. If there is a story in their creation, so much the better. These charming bird dishes, along with the gold-painted bamboo husks, were used at the second Tokyo Summit on May 5, 1986, attended by dignitaries including Japanese prime minister Yasuhiro Nakasone, U.S. president Ronald Reagan, British prime minister Margaret Thatcher, and French president François Mitterrand.

An example of a more recent creation can be seen in serving pieces designed by Kunio that were unveiled through his collaboration with the Western-style tableware manufacturer Okura Art China in 2008. *Flower Blizzard*, pictured on page 35, was the first in a series that brilliantly showcases, through tableware design paired with kaiseki cuisine, the Rimpa world of Kunio's vision.

LINKING SEASONAL HOLIDAYS AND EVENTS WITH CUISINE

In Japanese cuisine, especially kaiseki, using the tastiest seasonal fare at its peak is paramount. Going hand in hand with the best each season has to offer is a recognition of seasonal events, which adds yet another level of awareness and enjoyment to the meal.

Kyoto, above all, is known for its many traditional events and festivals. At Kitcho, these are celebrated with special décor and cuisine. The rituals behind such occasions have been handed down from generation to generation, many for hundreds of years, and form an ongoing thread throughout a person's lifetime. Some of the traditions are disappearing or evolving, yet they continue to resonate with diners, even more so when they are incorporated into the restaurant's repertoire with typical Kitcho flair.

This kaiseki course (above), served around the Doll Festival (Girl's Day) in early March, celebrates a special time for all female members of the family. Kitcho offers congratulatory sake to be drunk from the red-lacquered cup, and two dishes, *Goby and Egg Scramble* and *Assorted Spring Vegetables*, which are revealed (below) when the tops of the small ceramic dolls are lifted. A fine display of handcrafted dolls (right), created by a Kyoto doll maker around 1915, crowns the occasion.

Hassun Appetizers à la Rimpa. A vibrant bounty of abalone, shrimp, red ark clam, wild greens, and more is served in seashells—natural and ceramic—and the whole decorated with greens and flowering sprays.

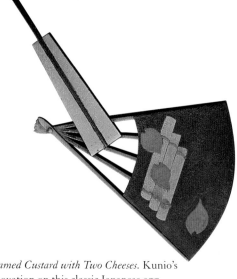

Steamed Custard with Two Cheeses. Kunio's innovation on this classic Japanese egg custard replaces the usual accents (pieces of shrimp, mushroom, chicken, and other tidbits) with creamy chunks of melting cheese. The parmesan grated on top hints at the rich, liquid surprise of the second cheese in the center.

One such holiday is the Doll Festival, which celebrates the health of young girls in early March—not only in Kyoto but across the entire country. People begin to observe this annual tradition in February by setting out decorative dolls, either large or small, for display in the home; the holiday culminates in a party with celebratory foods and drinks on March 3. Year after year, daughters are honored on this day, and wives and mothers can look back on the annual celebrations with fondness. Along with the ornamental dolls, sweet sake and peach blossoms are essential to the festivities. The tray on page 24 displays all three: a pair of small lidded dishes in the shape of husband-and-wife dolls, a petite red cup for sweet sake, and a twig with peach blossoms that does double duty as a chopstick rest. Removing the upper half of each doll reveals yet another course in a parade of foods conjured up for the holiday.

An equivalent celebration for boys takes place on May 5, when families hoist carp streamers, set out warrior dolls, and eat two kinds of traditional rice dumplings, among other foods.

Spring cuisine frequently makes use of wild greens such as the tender fronds of the ostrich fern, buds of the angelica tree, bracken, horsetail, and butterbur. For example,

RIGHT: *Arashiyama Cherry Blossoms* by Yamaguchi Soken (1759–1818). This hanging scroll offers a panoramic view of scenery in the vicinity of Kitcho, an area celebrated for its spring cherry blossoms and autumn colors. In the foreground is the famous Togetsukyo Bridge, which spans the Katsura River. The first bridge of that name went up around 840 A.D., but over the centuries it has been rebuilt many times. The current bridge dates from 1934.

Early morning cherry blossoms as seen from the second-story room Chidori. The garden at Kitcho boasts superb weeping cherry trees. When the blossoms begin to emerge in early spring, the Kitcho staff remove the screens so that guests can experience this world of mysterious beauty as fully as possible.

the covered bird dishes on page 17 contain tiny edible tree buds from the slender *koshiabura* tree (*Acanthopanax sciadophylloides*) and ostrich fern; the doll dishes on page 24 contain horsetail and ostrich fern; and the assorted spring greens on page 36 include bracken. Part of the appeal of these wild vegetables is their appearance and shape. There is also a desire to share in the vitality of these wild plants. The primary reason that they are so highly sought after, however, is that while all are tender and tasty if properly seasoned, they remain at heart untamed, with just a tinge of bitterness—one of the five essential flavors.

Kunio offers the following insight: "Animals waking from their winter sleep first nibble on bitter greens. Instinctively, they know that the bitterness helps the body eject the toxins that have built up during hibernation. In a word, they are participating in nature's detox program. Human physiology is no different." Young people's metabolism is so good that they have little physical need for bitterness, but as the years pile on, toxins tend to accumulate. With the edible wild greens that Kunio includes in his spring menus, diners can take advantage of nature's healthful detoxification benefits.

NATURE AND JAPANESE CUISINE

Of the many scenic attractions that draw people to Kyoto from across Japan and around the world, Arashiyama, where the main branch of the Kyoto Kitcho group is located, is among the most popular. "Arashiyama" is both the name of an area and the name of the mountain near Togetsukyo Bridge.

The appeal of the district lies in its scenic beauty and in the way the seasons unfold. Springtime is filled with cherry blossoms of every variety—mountain cherry, red weeping cherry, Somei Yoshino cherry, and more—and once the blossoms have passed, the vibrant green of new leaves conveys the vigor of life.

RIGHT: *Blossom-Viewing Picnic Lunch.* The delight of a *bento* lunch lies in its variety and portability. This one, made for outdoor cherry-blossom viewing, contains *Scattered Sushi* in the lower right compartment, along with more than a dozen rare morsels such as grilled scallops, red ark clam, salmon roe, and a delicious selection of wild greens.

Summer brings cormorant fishing and such refreshing seasonal activities as boating or strolling along the banks of the river. In fall, one can enjoy the bright colors of the changing leaves, a sky of glittering stars, and a silver moon hanging low above the edge of the mountain. Come winter, the hush of snow descends on river and mountains, on temple grounds and forests of bamboo.

These very aspects of nature—treasured for centuries—are reverently reflected in the cuisine at Kitcho. Seasonal motifs are an integral part of the serving ware (facing page and elsewhere), in the decoration—a spray of blossoms (pages 26–27) or a scattering of verdant leaves (page 44)—and in the countless inspirational acknowledgements of nature's bounty that appear throughout the course of a single meal. In short, nature, her seasons, and her abundance are celebrated and appreciated with endless inventiveness and joy.

IN PURSUIT OF FINE FLAVOR

Kunio makes this point often: "What do you think makes people happy? For one thing, eating. And why is that? Because enjoying good health fills us with happiness, and food is the single most important factor in maintaining good health."

He is concerned not only about the act of eating itself, but also about the importance of selecting cooking ingredients with the utmost care and then making the most of their potential. First, he actively seeks out organic, chemical-free produce, choosing growers whose produce is both safe and flavorful. Kunio is passionate about the need to cultivate and protect producers of "trustworthy" food.

The creation of mouthwatering cuisine requires using the best ingredients in the most effective way possible; this is Kunio's constant quest. As he puts it, "How can I make this dish even better?"

One of the fixtures of the Japanese garden is the stone basin known as a *tsukubai*, which generally features a slim bamboo pipe that feeds water into the basin. In this photo, cherry blossom petals that have fallen into the water from an overhanging branch are clustered along the sides of the basin. Such scenes inform much of Japanese culture and influence Kunio's food arrangements on many levels. The capriciousness of falling cherry blossoms helped inspire the plate design on the facing page.

The natural flavor of top-quality ingredients can be enhanced in any number of ways. For example, the cook may use a happy combination of two or more complementary flavors, as in the pairing of sea urchin and abalone. Or he may find new ways of drawing out a food's natural flavors before the cooking even begins. Or he might handle classic side dishes in an unexpected way that raises the culinary bar. Kunio constantly pushes boundaries, asking himself if the accepted way of doing things is necessarily the best way. He starts by questioning every aspect and reexamining every step, then experiments with new methods until he comes up with a better approach. With his extraordinary curiosity, patience, and talent, he makes it look easy.

Kunio's treatment of *nori* seaweed is one such example. Sheets of toasted *nori* are always used for wrapping rice balls. The method of toasting the *nori* to bring out the flavor and fragrance has been passed down from mother to daughter for generations in the kitchens of Japan, and the same method is inscribed in cookbooks throughout the land: "Press together two sheets of *nori* with the top sides

RIGHT: *Beef and Vegetable Sushi.* Lightly seared slices of prime beef take the place of fish in this version of the Japanese classic. To stand up to the heartier meat flavor, stir-fried minced onion, shiitake mushroom, and wild greens are mixed into the rice, creating a subtle explosion of tastes.

facing inward, and toast the rougher undersides." The process is so basic and traditional that it is ingrained in the Japanese psyche. But through experimentation, Kunio found that toasting the opposite side, the so-called top side, leads to more desirable results. For one thing, the underside is bumpy and inclined to scorch, leading to a deterioration in taste, however subtle. His logic is unquestionable.

Likewise, Kunio grates the Japanese horseradish known as wasabi, an essential complement for sashimi and sushi, after his own fashion rather than according to tradition. The standard approach calls for the cook to "start near the leaves and continue grating from there," but Kunio grates his wasabi from both ends of the root, taking equal amounts from the leafy end and the tip, then mixing them. Why? Because the sweetness, pungency, and refreshing coolness of the wasabi are all stronger at the base of the root, growing weaker toward the tip. Kunio's method creates an ideal balance of flavor—another incremental change in tradition that further enhances the overall quality of the cuisine at Kitcho.

Perhaps his most groundbreaking innovation is his recipe for *dashi* stock (see page 171), a key element in Japanese cuisine. The excellence of the *dashi* determines the depth of flavor of a chef's food. The *dashi* depends on the quality of kelp and dried bonito flakes and the method of making the stock.

Broadly speaking, virtually every Japanese chef—Teiichi included—has always followed the same method of making *dashi*. First, the kelp is placed in a pan of cold water and heated over a low flame. When the kelp begins to stir, it is removed and replaced with bonito shavings. Simple, elegant and easily accepted. But Kunio takes matters a step further, leaving the kelp to soak, unheated, for sixteen hours. In this way, he coaxes a better flavor from the kelp, and achieves a more subtle base stock from which to start. He then removes the kelp, heats the stock, and adds bonito shavings.

The process sounds easy enough, but Kunio only settled on this method after repeated experimentation in his unending search for the fullest flavors. Over time, he pondered the qualities of kelp and dried bonito. He ran endless experiments, changing the variables incrementally. How does heating protein change its flavor? What precise change does the flavor undergo? What temperature is ideal for maximizing flavor? While these and other questions will be explored in a later section, the point worth noting here is that Kunio's persistent drive to seek out the full potential of each and every ingredient that passes through his kitchen sets him apart from the crowd.

YUKI MUSEUM OF ART

Near the Kitahama area of Osaka, a major financial center, is an oasis of calm: the Yuki Museum of Art. Opened in November 1987, the museum displays culinary vessels and tea utensils collected and cherished by Teiichi Yuki. But Teiichi did not establish the museum out of a desire to display his superb

BELOW: *Mélange of Spring Greens.* Delicacies are mounded in an elegant blue-and-white porcelain bowl: Venus clams in batter add a counterpoint to spring cabbage, snap peas, bracken, long onions, and Japanese pumpkin, dressed in a creamy sauce of daikon radish, onion, kelp stock, and butter.

collection. He assembled the items for display in the first place not as high-end art objects but as beloved objects for practical use and enjoyment; and he did, in fact, use them. Only when the collection appreciated well beyond the point where everyday use became impractical did he put it on display, though he continued to acquire pieces for the restaurant.

He also wanted to continue to share his favorite possessions. "If you make a good livelihood by serving fine cuisine, it's important to give something back to your customers for their enjoyment." This was Teiichi's firm belief. At his restaurant, and during the tea ceremonies he conducted, he used the items he collected: he arranged food in the vessels, decorated alcoves with the hanging scrolls, set flowers in the vases. He believed that using an item imbues it with life.

The idea of setting up a museum arose spontaneously among his fellow tea masters. "The number of people who can attend a tea ceremony or a dinner is limited," they pointed out. "These tea things and the rest ought to be known more widely." This advice gives some indication of just how valuable and extraordinary Teiichi's collection had become. Moreover, it would have been a shame had any of the pieces been broken or damaged in everyday use, and surely his friends also saw the need for a museum as a place where the collection could be safely maintained.

In all, the museum houses hundreds of pieces, including eleven Important Cultural Properties and another three Important Art Objects. Serving ware that Kunio has used for his culinary creations include a Jingdezhen porcelain bowl from the late Ming dynasty (second half of the seventeenth century, page 36); a series of eighteenth-century cylindrical appetizer vessels by Ogata Kenzan (pages 46–47); and a seventeenth-century Oribe rectangular dish with handle that has been designated an Important Cultural Property (page 107). These centuries-old objects have been handed down for generations and ended up in Kunio's care. Each one possesses a commanding dignity, creating a strong presence all its own. At the same time, the pieces radiate a gentleness born of the love and use that the previous owners, including Teiichi, lavished on them over the ages.

Giant stalks of bamboo. Each spring, when the pale shoots poke through the ground covering, they must be unearthed and collected. The harvested portion is surprisingly long, ranging from 10 to 12 inches (25 to 30 cm) or longer, and more than 4 inches (10 cm) in diameter at the thickest point.

BAMBOO SHOOTS—Attention to Cultivation and Cooking

Bamboo shoots are a representative spring vegetable in Kyoto. They are tender and savory, yielding their delicate flavor to the diner's palate at the merest

Bamboo Shoot Mélange. Decorated with elegant motifs of spring and fall to represent time's eternal flow, this bowl offers up freshly harvested bamboo shoots, a crisp and tender delicacy, cooked three different ways.

Whole Grilled Bamboo Shoots. Leaving fresh shoots in their husks as they cook allows them to steam in their own juices, amplifying their natural sweetness and satisfyingly firm texture.

pressure. There are many varieties of bamboo in Japan, but Kitcho uses the feathery *mosochiku* exclusively, and only the choicest specimens grown locally and in monitored conditions.

Incidentally, the link between Kitcho and bamboo is both epicurean and geographical. The Arashiyama district remains home to a great forest of bamboo that is a major scenic attraction in Kyoto. A bamboo grove has pleasant associations, and is another facet of nature much appreciated in Japan. The green of the bamboo is refreshing and the wind in the leaves produces a pleasant rustling sound. In fact, a list of "One Hundred Japanese Soundscapes Worth Preserving" selected by the Ministry of the Environment includes the bamboo groves in Sagano and Rakusei, adjacent to Arashiyama.

Even in dense bamboo forests, young shoots appear in the spring. But the shoots used in the restaurant are harvested not from the wild but from fields of bamboo cultivated for that purpose. The bamboo stalks are planted at wide intervals. The soil is turned over frequently and is so springy that anyone stepping into it would likely sink up to the calf. This springiness is what gives bamboo shoots grown here their characteristic tenderness. Fertilizer, too, is carefully chosen with an eye to improving flavor. Bamboo shoots are harvested in April and May, and the rest of the year is spent tending the fields. Groves left to themselves cannot produce shoots of comparable quality.

With bamboo shoots, freshness is of paramount importance. The shoots appear suddenly and without notice, so when a bamboo grower telephones with the news that he is about to dig some up, the kitchen staff quickly set vats of water to boil. When the shoots arrive, they are rinsed off and plunged straight into boiling water. The more time passes after they are harvested, the more astringent they become, so it is vital to boil them as quickly as possible.

Japanese Risotto. For this flavorful risotto with a Japanese flair, the rice is first cooked in olive oil like a true risotto, then simmered in a kelp stock. Garnishes of bonito flakes, seasoned bonito and kelp bits, and minced rape blossom are added along the way.

RIGHT: Garden path at one of Kitcho's tea houses.

FAR RIGHT, TOP: *Rice Topped with Egg and Tempura.* Kunio gently sets slivers of tender egg, whitebait tempura, and greens on a bed of fragrant short-grain Japanese rice.

FAR RIGHT, BOTTOM: *Sea Bream Chazuke.* This surprisingly savory Japanese dish combines rice with a lightly salted green-tea "soup base," topped with fresh sea bream, sesame-paste balls, wasabi, and *nori* seaweed.

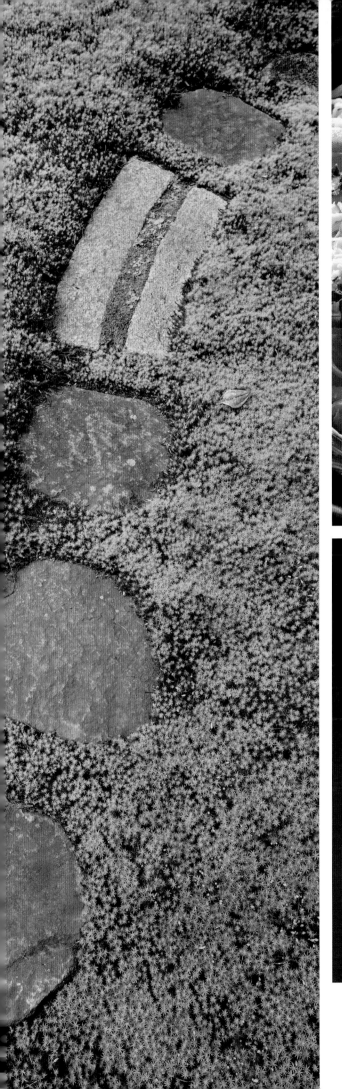

Kunio's approach to sweets is as innovative as his take on savory courses. Although the *Cherry Blossom Rice Dumpling* (top) is fairly traditional, he sweetens the *Bracken Dumpling* (middle) with an import, maple sugar. He then reverses direction, adding a Japanese accent to a Western dessert in his *Green Tea Tiramisu with Mascarpone,* where the addition of *matcha*, the powdered green tea of the tea ceremony, lends the dessert a rich, slightly bitter taste that reflects the kaiseki cuisine served at Kitcho.

Bamboo plays a variety of roles at Kitcho. Aside from holding a cherished place in the cuisine, it shows up in decorative elements and utensils as well. The pan-roasted rice balls on page 15 are placed in a gilded bamboo husk. The fresh green ring of bamboo on page 79 keeps summer noodles separate from their sauce until the diner releases them. On page 82 is a bamboo vase fashioned by Shoan, a protégé of sixteenth-century tea master Sen no Rikyu. The bamboo tea scoop on page 151 was carved by Rikyu himself. After four hundred years, the once-green bamboo used for the vase and scoop has taken on an amber patina with the sheen of fine lacquer.

THE FINISHING TOUCH—GREEN TEA AND SWEETS

A kaiseki meal begins with appetizers and ends with rice, followed by fruit. After such a sumptuous meal, one wants to linger in the moment, enjoying the haze of satisfaction unique to a fine repast.

The perfect interlude at such times is a serving of frothy, fragrant green tea—whipped from the powdered tea known as *matcha*—accompanied by a sweet that evokes the season or some seasonal festivity. Fortunately, Kyoto is home to three major tea ceremony schools and so boasts a great many confectionery shops, including some that are centuries old. While all the sweets served at Kitcho are made on the premises, chefs are in the unique position of being able to draw upon the generations of knowledge and refinement that surround them at every turn.

The designs of Nonomura Ninsei, one of Kyoto's most renowned potters, are known for their elegance and expressive artistry. This refined seventeenth-century tea bowl is decorated with three fans in overglaze enamels of red, blue, green, purple, and gold on a characteristic cream-colored earthenware body. Ritsuko Tokuoka, Kunio's wife and the gracious *okami*, or proprietress, of Kitcho, served guests thin whipped green tea (*usucha*) from this bowl at her wedding reception.

"Some of our sweets suggest seasonal flowers, or highlight a scene from nature, such as flowing water," explains Kunio. "Others are associated with a particular event, and so we serve them just one day out of the year. In addition, customers sometimes request something special for a personal celebration. As we make all these sweets by hand, our confectionery production alone adds up to a huge number of recipes over the course of a year."

Just as Kunio incorporates nontraditional ingredients such as beef and parmesan cheese into Japanese cuisine, he is similarly adventuresome in his approach to sweets. For the *Bracken Dumpling* in the center of the facing page, Kunio uses a very nontraditional sweetener, maple sugar. He also reverses the effect: the *Green Tea Tiramisu with Mascarpone* shown at the bottom adds a distinctive Japanese accent to a Western-style dessert.

With each dessert comes the tea, in a tea bowl made to be used in the tea ceremony. At Kitcho, they serve the beverage in high-quality tea bowls by top artist-potters. In Teiichi's time, the priceless Ninsei bowl on this page or the Ido bowl on page 121 were sometimes used for special occasions. But the price of older pieces such as these has soared to hundreds of thousands of dollars, so they are brought out only rarely these days, if at all. But rest assured, a newer generation of classic serving bowls has replaced the older generation, and the quality is unchanged.

ON THE JAPANESE SENSE OF BEAUTY AND
INNOVATION IN THE KITCHEN

As one peruses the images, writing, and food to this point, Kunio's Rimpa style of cooking comes into focus. His is a creative, intuitive way of working, and at times grasping the essentials of his work requires a willingness to stand back, watch, listen, and allow images and ideas and tastes, real and imagined, to penetrate.

Expanding on the comparison between his cooking and the inventive Japanese painting style of old, Kunio says, "Rimpa didn't spring out of nowhere. It came about naturally, just as painting styles from earlier centuries were adapted to suit the needs of later ages. Rimpa emerged to fill a need of the time and as an expression of the time. That's what Rimpa is. In the same way, I have my own style of expression, one that's naturally suited to the times I live in. I think there's room for a personal style that can blend in with contemporary times without deviating from the history of Japanese cuisine, in which my grandfather Teiichi played a part."

Kunio's style is also evident in the serving dishes he has designed. One aspect of the Japanese sense of beauty is an affinity for asymmetry, in contrast to the Western preference for symmetry. The plate on page 35, for example, is decorated with a scattering of cherry blossoms that is at once random and natural, yet highly stylized. Some of the petals spill over the rim of the plate, echoing the way real blossoms fall. Kunio takes pleasure in such spilling across boundaries, and in patterns found in nature, like the random clustering of petals in the stone washbasin on page 34. "Cherry petals float in a washbasin without pattern, just as they are flung about by a passing breeze. As I look at them, other petals drift down from branches overhead. I see beauty in such scenes."

There is another aspect to Kunio's appreciation of nature. He, like many Japanese, sees beauty not just in the perfectly formed blossom but also in

Plump bites of shrimp, octopus, and other delicacies dangling from thin bamboo skewers show an airy playfulness in keeping with Kunio's Rimpa style and his sense of adventure—an appropriate nod to renowned artist-potter Ogata Kenzan, who produced more eating vessels than he did tea ceremony ware. These distinctive appetizer vessels are from a set of ten that feature designs of cranes, reeds, bracken, orchids, pine, and other traditional motifs in glazes of cobalt blue and iron.

its various stages of life. For the arrangement on page 82 he chose magnolia buds instead of blooming flowers. The buds seem ready to open at any moment, and this stimulates the viewer's imagination. It creates anticipation, allows the mind to make leaps. "For tea occasions I prefer flowers that are on the verge of opening, or ones that are past their prime and ready to scatter their petals. Many people in Japan also appreciate the beauty of such moments."

These sentiments, which infuse Kunio's way of working, have their roots in Zen and the tea ceremony. Teiichi was a noted tea master, and Kunio, from the time he was a small boy in primary school, used to drink *matcha* (the dense green powdered tea used in the ceremony) whenever he could. During childhood, he was sent to a Zen temple for summer vacations, which is how he first encountered the tea ceremony and discovered the deep connection between Zen and tea. At age twenty, he decided to formally study the tea ceremony, convinced that to understand Teiichi he needed to immerse himself in the world of tea.

Paradoxically, this absorption of the very traditional spirit of the tea ceremony may be what enables Kunio to use nontraditional ingredients to create a world that is indubitably Japanese. Examples of his wizardry include the *Beef and Vegetable Sushi* on page 35, where he replaces fish with tender slices of beef; and the *Steamed Custard with Two Cheeses* on page 28, where cheese is used to startling effect. Incorporating cheese in this traditional dish, which dates back to the mid-eighteenth century, is a striking innovation. The tender softness of broth-flavored egg custard combines with melting cheese inside and out for a rich, savory taste that is light, yet satisfying. In his daring willingness to fully showcase the inosinic acid in both cheeses, Kunio once again reveals the brilliance of his Rimpa style.

SUMMER KAISEKI

Hot Blanched Pike Conger presents an iconic Kyoto delicacy, which is seasoned, lightly boiled, and served hot. Though blanched pike conger is usually chilled, this preparation brings out the full flavor of the fish.

NEAR RIGHT: The well-tended ground under the eaves outside the Taikotei dining room is a sophisticated arrangement of pebbles, stones, and raked sand to catch the rain run-off from the tiled roof—a harmony of colors and forms as beautiful as it is functional.

KYOTO AND PIKE CONGER—A Cherished Seasonal Delicacy

A summer and early autumn food that Kyotoites dearly love is pike conger, or *hamo* in Japanese. There is even a saying that a Kyoto summer without pike conger is unthinkable. The Gion Festival (see page 62) wouldn't be the same without *Pike Conger Pressed Sushi*, in which pike conger broiled with a sweet sauce is pressed onto vinegared sushi rice. So strong is the association between the old capital city and this delicacy that the haiku poet Takarai Kikaku penned a wistful piece more than three hundred years ago: "Pike conger on sushi— / how I long to be there now / in the capital."

But Kyoto is cut off from the sea, and so for much of its history, until an efficient distribution system came into place, the ancient capital lacked direct access to seafood. How then did pike conger dishes become such an important local specialty? The answer to this riddle lies in the fish's amazing hardiness. Pike congers captured live in the Seto Inland Sea could be transported to the capital in twenty-four hours without perishing. On top of this all-important vitality, the pike conger has a delicately flavored white meat that blends exquisitely with its savory fatty layer. For Kyoto residents, eating pike conger became an essential way to survive the oppressive summer heat.

Enter the kitchen at Kitcho during the summertime and you're sure to hear the steady *chop-chop-chop* of knives moving softly but swiftly across the cutting block. This is the sound of pike conger—bones and all—being chopped. The pike conger is known for its countless tiny bones, too numerous to be removed. Instead, the fish is cut in three portions and laid skin-side down on a carving board. The bones are then chopped with a carving knife at tiny intervals, amounting to twenty-five cuts or more per inch, while never cutting through the skin—a fiendishly difficult challenge for anyone who hasn't mastered the art. Young cooks pool their money to buy pike congers to practice on.

Pike conger starts tasting best around the onset of the rainy season in early summer. "The season runs from around mid-June till October," explains Kunio. "Because the season's so long, the vegetables we use in combination with the fish gradually change. It's an ingredient that can be enjoyed in a rich variety of ways."

This *Basket of Hassun Morsels* sweeps aside the oppressive summer heat with its elegant combination of Baccarat crystal and crushed ice, on which seasoned greens, simmered fish, and more are set in a finely crafted bamboo basket.

This book presents two dishes that feature pike conger: *Hot Blanched Pike Conger* (page 51) and *Pike Conger and Matsutake Mushroom Bowl* (page 115), featuring late-season pike congers and fresh *matsutake* mushrooms. Along with dishes like *Pike Conger Pressed Sushi*, pike conger hot pots are popular: *Pike Conger Shabu-Shabu*, in which raw morsels are cooked at the table by dipping them quickly into hot, light broth; *Pike Conger Sukiyaki*, featuring the fish meat simmered in a richly flavored broth, sukiyaki style; and *Pike Conger Yanagawa*, where fish meat and burdock are simmered together and the flavor sealed in with beaten egg.

Hot Blanched Pike Conger is a Kunio original. Traditionally, pike conger is blanched in hot water, then plunged into ice water and served cold as a refreshing treat. "But putting it in ice water turns the skin rubbery," says Kunio. "I don't like it that way myself. I decided it was more important for my guests to appreciate the full umami of the soft skin than it was for them to enjoy the chilled fish in summertime. That's how I came up with the idea of serving it hot."

Even for diners who enjoy the traditional dish, the hot version offers a revelation: besides the light and tender fish meat, there is also the singular flavor of the skin to enjoy. Such innovations come about through Kunio's constant search for ways to improve flavor, unhampered by fixed ideas even when it comes to classic, nostalgia-laden dishes.

Always a luxury food, in recent years pike conger has become even more extravagant. At the same time, it is becoming more widely sought; no longer unique to the Kansai area and Kyushu, it has become increasingly popular with Tokyo chefs as well, and even shows up in French cuisine.

THE *HASSUN* COURSE AT KITCHO—Awakening Body and Mind

The word *hassun* means literally "eight *sun*," a traditional Japanese measurement equal to about 9½ inches (24 cm)—the length of the plain square wooden tray used in olden times to make offerings of *umi no mono* (seafood) and *yama no mono* (mountain foods) to Shinto gods. Over time, the word came to refer to the delicacies themselves, then to a course featuring these foods in a formal kaiseki meal.

A Kitcho *hassun* course, conceived and arranged with the utmost care, is epitomized by the *Basket of Hassun Morsels* (facing page), with flowers enhancing a colorful array of tantalizing delicacies, here in a serving for three. *Hassun* courses also appear on pages 26–27, 75, 76–77, 100–101, 104–105, 128–129, and 140.

Kunio sometimes starts with the *hassun* course, but sometimes puts it midway through the meal, a change that naturally affects the role the course plays in the meal. He explains, "A *hassun* at the start of the meal serves mainly to whet guests' appetites and rouse their curiosity. When it comes in the middle of the meal, after the initial novelty of the occasion has worn off, visual impact is important as a way to refresh people and liven things up." Either way, the *hassun* course awakens body and mind while raising anticipation. Clearly, it is a fundamental factor in assuring guests' enjoyment of the kaiseki experience.

But that is only the beginning of its role. "Visual impact is particularly important in the *hassun* course," says Kunio. "I arrange flowers and foods to make a visual statement about the season while also paying attention to flavors, colors,

The Zangetsu (Lingering Moon) room is airy and inviting, decked out in light summer fittings of woven bamboo. From the room and hall, diners have a refreshing view of garden verdure through glass sliding doors.

and style. I go to great pains to maintain a balance. Sometimes aroma is important, sometimes texture—a lot of elements besides flavor come into play. In China, the ancient five-elements theory is reflected in cuisine, so there's a traditional emphasis on five flavors, five colors, five directions, and five cooking methods. I would add one more: the five senses."

The five flavors Kunio works with are sweet, sour, bitter, salty, and savory. In Chinese tradition, the fifth flavor is spicy, but he believes spiciness counts as stimulation, not true flavor. "Ideally speaking, in every dish in a full-course meal, each element should be present in a balanced way, making a harmonious, integrated whole. I carefully plan the ingredients, structure, and order of every item on the menu to make that happen."

Kunio says, "In essence, *hassun* represents not just the abundance of sea and land but all the phenomena of nature and the universe. It's in that spirit that guests are offered contrasting delicacies, one from the sea and one from the land, on a simple tray."

Splashing ladlefuls of water around the entrance and garden is a traditional way to make the area ready for guests; it also eases the heat.

The *hassun* course originated with the meal accompanying a tea ceremony, and Teiichi adapted the concept to his kitchens when he created modern kaiseki. In the spirit of tea, where guests are treated with as much respect as the gods, Teiichi incorporated flowers and other beautiful offerings from nature into his *hassun* presentations, and developed ways of presenting delicacies from sea, mountain, river, and land in a highly visual format. Today, Kunio is actively extending and building on this tradition.

CREATING COOLNESS IN SUMMER: Décor and Utensils

Kyoto's location in a valley basin means that in summer, temperatures and humidity skyrocket. Kitcho is out in Arashiyama, where hills and mountains keep temperatures noticeably cooler than in the downtown area, yet even there by June the sliding paper doors and screens used in wintertime must be exchanged for doors and screens of woven bamboo or reeds (pages 54–55) that allow the air to circulate more freely. This changeover is by no means a simple process; the job takes all morning and requires an all-out effort from everyone, including the office staff and cooking staff. It is in fact an important annual event marking the change of seasons. Once the replacement is complete, the rooms are transformed, becoming refreshingly light, summery, and cool.

Many other touches help to make Kitcho cool and pleasant in summer. During the months from May to October, when portable stoves are used for boiling water to make tea, the rooms are scented with light, aromatic sandalwood in place of the incense briquettes used in winter. Flowers, moreover, are arranged in flat, shallow containers so that the water in them is visible, further heightening the impression of coolness.

All sorts of pains are taken to ensure guests' comfort despite the heat. "We bring out linen cushion covers," says Kunio's wife Ritsuko. "And the tea cups we set out for guests when they first arrive are crystal—not porcelain—filled with iced green tea. We make sure the gardens are kept moist by sprinkling them with water frequently, too."

In the old days, people endured the summer heat just by fanning themselves and by changing room fittings to visually suggest coolness. In modern times, air conditioning is also unobtrusively used to provide relief from summer's stifling heat.

■ ■ ■

Another important element in ensuring guests' comfort in summer is of course the selection of utensils and food containers, mainly featuring vessels made of crystal glassware or an arrangement using ice.

Nearly all of the crystal utensils at Kitcho are antique French Baccarat, which suggest a crisp coolness while lending a bright sparkle to the table. Among the Baccarat creations are the gold-rimmed sake cups in *Basket of Hassun Morsels* (page 52), the soup bowls used in *Cold Turtle Soup* (facing page), the small gold-rimmed bowls adorned with reed circles for the shrimp and mushroom dish on page 61, and the square dish used for *Grilled Summer Vegetables* (page 65). Some of these pieces were fashioned in the early twentieth century for a dealer in Osaka and later acquired by Teiichi. The rest were made to order for Kunio, according to his specifications.

At Kitcho, crystal utensils come in all varieties, including sake decanters, sake cups, and tumblers for other alcoholic beverages; medium-sized plates and square platters; boats; square bowls; lidded soup bowls; and so on. "It's possible to serve a full-course meal using only crystal," says Kunio, "but that wouldn't appeal to the Japanese sense of beauty. It's much more effective to suggest coolness by mixing crystal with, say, Shigaraki pottery that's been dipped in water and is still wet, or blue celadon suggestive of water, or something in a refreshing blue-and-white porcelain."

Ice is also sometimes used as a serving surface. From the moment it's brought to the table, ice lends its coolness to the surrounding air in a delightful way. Containers may be filled with crushed ice (pages 52, 61, 75, 76–77), or the container itself made from ice (page 63). The *Octopus Triad* is served in a hollowed globe of ice called an "ice balloon." Such touches inject a pleasurable note of playfulness into the meal. Ice-caves (*kamakura*) and trays made of finely chipped ice also find their way into the parade of courses at Kitcho.

An old Japanese saying goes, "In summer, coolness is as delicious as fine food." This maxim carries great weight at Kitcho.

The golden yellow hue of *Cold Turtle Soup* is a visual harbinger of the marvelous flavor of this extravagant soup, which has a full-bodied umami unique to well-tended snapping turtles brought up on white-fleshed fish.

TURTLE—A Neglected Ingredient

Opinions are invariably divided when it comes to turtle meat. Many diners see turtle as a bizarre food choice, one they'd prefer to steer clear of. Yet turtle cuisine is truly gourmet fare, as one mouthful of *Cold Turtle Soup* (page 58) is enough to make clear. This refined and richly savory soup is sure to win over skeptics and make them regret having denied themselves such pleasure in the past.

The peculiarly intense flavor sometimes associated with turtle meat is the result of the animal's omnivorous diet. Snapping turtles served at Kitcho, however, are fed only white-flesh fish, and are raised carefully in a clean environment. The meat of these specially bred turtles is delicious, with no hint of gaminess. Its main appeal is indeed its flavor. Different from the oily richness of prime beef, the clear fat exudes a distinctive, satisfying flavor that combines the full-bodied taste of dark-meat chicken and the finest white-flesh fish.

"And then there's the feel of it in your mouth, too," says Kunio. "When turtle meat is simmered, it forms a gelatin with a wonderful springy texture. There's just nothing like it."

The most typical way of serving turtle is in a stew filled with chunks of tender meat. Indeed, so entrenched is the stew that Kyoto even has a specialty restaurant that has continued to serve nothing but turtle stew throughout the year for over three centuries. People who are fond of the meat may not be able to enjoy it as often as they wish, however, since it's now a luxury food item. Back when Tokyo was known as Edo, turtle meat was widely accessible. The downtown Akasaka district still has a neighborhood called Tameike ("reservoir") where there once was a reservoir inhabited by large numbers of snapping turtles—an inexpensive, plentiful source of the meat.

At Kitcho, *Cold Turtle Soup* has been a staple on the menu from the first, but Kunio insists another way of cooking turtle is even better: "You've got to eat it salt-grilled in the fall." The flavor deepens in late autumn, when turtles eat enormous amounts as they prepare for winter hibernation. "The taste is mild, but at the same time it has unbelievable depth. Our guests react with amazement and delight." This is one of Kunio's surprising culinary masterpieces.

ABOVE: A fan with a design from the leadoff float in the famed Gion Festival. Every July, Kitcho displays one of these sought-after fans for guests' enjoyment.

RIGHT: A screen painting of the Tsuki Hoko float, one of the most lavish in the festival, celebrating the Shinto god of the moon.

Shrimp, Grilled Shiitake, and Water Shield Leaf in Tosa Vinegar combines fresh seafood and vegetables in a light vinaigrette. The reed rings that decorate this dish recall a traditional summer rite.

LINKING CUISINE WITH ANNUAL RITUAL

Just as Girl's Day comes in spring, summer, too, brings traditional events in the cycle of life in Japan, and each celebration has its customarily associated dishes. In July, the music of the Gion Festival reverberates around Kyoto, and the joyful sound of bells, drums, and flutes fills the ancient capital with excitement. This great festival, which includes prayers at Yasaka Shrine for protection from epidemics, actually has a 1,100-year history.

Kunio explains: "Famine, epidemics, and other troubles would periodically visit the capital, and people could only wonder why. The festival got started as a way for people to make offerings to the gods, pray for an end to sickness, and cheer themselves up." Such events soon became a part of the peoples' lives.

Every year, hundreds of thousands of sightseers flock to Kyoto for Yoiyama, the nighttime display of floats on July 16, followed by a grand parade the next day. Thirty-two tall, colorful floats weighing some ten tons each, many of them decorated with superb old and new tapestries from countries east and west, proceed from the Shijo-Karasuma intersection along main city streets. The elegant spectacle is greeted by appreciative cheers and bursts of applause all along the route.

In the spring of 2009, a wave of H1N1 influenza caused a dramatic drop in the number of visitors to the city. Kyotoites feared that the Gion Festival would fail to attract its usual crowds, but cheered each other up by saying "All the more reason to go to Yasaka Shrine and pray for good health!" Though to outsiders the festival may be an occasion of dazzling splendor and magnificence, to locals it is inextricably woven into their life. The festival has remained an occasion to offer prayers for protection from sickness, a practice unchanged in essence from a millennium ago.

The Gion Festival is one of Japan's three great festivals, the other two being Tokyo's Kanda Festival in mid-May and Osaka's Tenjin Festival in late July. Interestingly, each one is associated with a particular food. Pike conger or *hamo* (see pages 50–53), an indispensible part of summer in Kyoto, is strongly associated with the Gion Festival. The fish's natural vitality is held to be an excellent cure for the summer listlessness caused by brutal heat and humidity, enabling those who eat it to keep up their strength and stave off illness. At the Kanda Festival, people eat "red festival rice" (*sekihan*) and shredded squid boiled in a sweet broth (*kiri-ika*), while at Tenjin Festival the specialty is vinegared octopus.

■ ■ ■

Shrimp, Grilled Shiitake, and Water Shield Leaf in Tosa Vinegar (page 61) is served in connection with the summer purification rite held at shrines across the city on June 30. Inside the shrine precincts are huge circles called *chinowa*, made of

Old-style traditional umbrellas made of oiled paper and bamboo are lined up in readiness for staff to shelter guests when it rains.

RIGHT: Before diners take a single bite, they are refreshed by the very sight of the ice balloon that holds the *Octopus Triad*. Tender bits of octopus are sautéed; deep-fried; or blanched, chilled, and dotted with pickled-apricot paste.

miscanthus reed. Visitors step through these to rid themselves of defilement and impurities accumulated in the first six months of the year, while praying for safe passage through the remainder of the year.

The dish is served caged with miscanthus rings in a playful reference to this custom. Diners eat it by inserting their chopsticks through a miscanthus circle to grasp the shrimp and other dainties. "This way at least the fingertips pass through," says Kunio. "It's our expression of sincere wishes for guests' continued health and happiness." The paper talismans that bind the rings are not merely decorative, but were actually purified at nearby Nonomiya Shrine.

HERBS AND SPICES

The great cooking traditions of the world, such as French, Italian, Thai, and Vietnamese cuisines, all use a variety of herbs and spices. Parsley, thyme, rosemary, laurel, dill, and mint are only a few of the cooking herbs commonly used, which easily number over one hundred. Japanese cuisine, too, has its herbs and spices of long standing: for spring, young sprigs and buds of the Japanese prickly ash (*kinome* and *hanazansho*); and for summer, water pepper (*tade*), prickly ash berries and the buds, seedlings, and leaves of perilla (*shiso*, also called beefsteak plant or Japanese basil), as well as myoga ginger (which has a more subtle, fainter taste than regular ginger); and for winter, dropwort and trefoil. Flavor enhancers used year-round include welsh onion and other onion varieties, wasabi, ginger, ground seedpods of prickly ash (*sansho*), and *bainiku*, a tangy paste made from the sieved flesh of salt-pickled Japanese apricot (*umeboshi*).

Traditional flavor combinations provide essential finishing touches in Japanese cuisine, although they are few in number. The young leaves of prickly ash are used in dishes closely reflecting seasonality, and figure prominently in *Bamboo Shoot Mélange* (page 39). Pickled-apricot paste is *de rigueur* with pike conger; in *Hot Blanched Pike Conger* (page 51), the scarlet dabs make a bright contrast. The green herb sprinkled on *Sweetfish Rice* (page 78) is finely chopped water pepper (*tade*), a traditional taste partner for sweetfish. *Salt-Grilled Sweetfish* (pages 70–71) is enjoyed with a dipping sauce of vinegar mixed with water pepper. Both prickly ash sprigs and water pepper provide piquant pungency.

RIGHT: *Grilled Summer Vegetables* features lotus root, green peppers, Japanese pumpkin (*kabocha*), and eggplant, basted with a *dashi*-based sauce and topped with myoga ginger.

Foods that play a supporting role have the function of adding zest while deepening the inherent flavor of the main food. For rich, hearty fare, the accompaniment should have a pleasantly cleansing effect on the palate. *Clear Chicken Kelp Soup* (page 22), for example, is served with spring onion prepared in two different ways, shredded and grilled. *Cabbage and Horse Mackerel Mille-Feuille* (above right) is garnished with perilla buds and slivered ginger, while the accompaniments for *Grilled Eel Uzaku* (facing page) are slivered perilla leaf and myoga ginger mixed with shredded cabbage. The myoga ginger in *Grilled Summer Vegetables* (page 65) and the perilla leaf and pickled-apricot paste in *Lotus Rice* (page 79) serve to draw together the flavors of the whole.

"In summer I use lots and lots of perilla," says Kunio. "It's so light and refreshing. Myoga ginger I never use by itself, but in summer and early fall it's indispensable. The aroma and texture are beyond words."

FAR LEFT: *Eggplant and Baby Red Shrimp.* Eggplant, a popular summer food, is briskly deep-fried, then braised in a *dashi*-based sauce. The shrimp is deep-fried until crisp, offering a crunchy counterpart to the eggplant's softness.

LEFT: *Cabbage and Horse Mackerel Mille-Feuille.* Salt-softened cabbage leaves and mackerel are layered, then allowed to macerate before being topped with perilla buds and finely shredded ginger, refreshing garnishes.

RIGHT: Eel, another favorite summer food, is offered in this *Grilled Eel Uzaku.* The eel is dressed in a sweet sauce and accompanied by an appetizing combination of shredded cabbage, slivered myoga ginger, and perilla leaves, all rubbed lightly with salt and cured in kelp *dashi*. Ginger triangles marinated in sweetened vinegar add the final touch.

Fragrant citron (*yuzu*) is also used extensively in Japanese cooking across the seasons, from the white flowers of spring to the green fruit of summer and the yellow fruit of late fall. *Pike Conger and Matsutake Mushroom Bowl* (page 115), a fall dish, is sprinkled with grated peel of green citron, while in *Genji Inkstone Lid Hassun* (pages 104–105), a hollowed yellow citron is used as a serving vessel.

Strangely enough—or perhaps not so strangely—nature has arranged matters so that foods with complementary flavors come into season at the same time. When bamboo shoots are at their best, so are aromatic prickly ash sprigs; the same holds true for sweetfish and water pepper, as well as eel or horse mackerel and perilla buds or myoga ginger. Perhaps the greatest contribution of herbs to Japanese cooking is the way they heighten our awareness of the season through such exquisite harmonies.

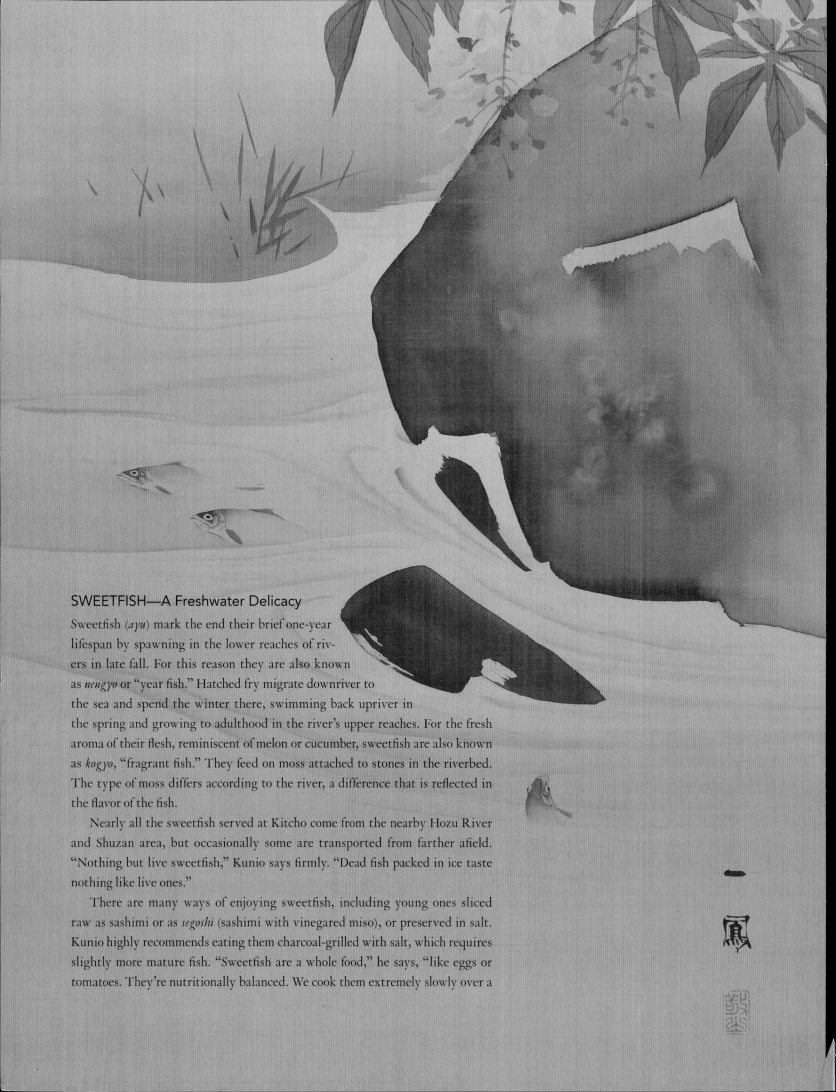

SWEETFISH—A Freshwater Delicacy

Sweetfish (*ayu*) mark the end their brief one-year lifespan by spawning in the lower reaches of rivers in late fall. For this reason they are also known as *nengyo* or "year fish." Hatched fry migrate downriver to the sea and spend the winter there, swimming back upriver in the spring and growing to adulthood in the river's upper reaches. For the fresh aroma of their flesh, reminiscent of melon or cucumber, sweetfish are also known as *kogyo*, "fragrant fish." They feed on moss attached to stones in the riverbed. The type of moss differs according to the river, a difference that is reflected in the flavor of the fish.

Nearly all the sweetfish served at Kitcho come from the nearby Hozu River and Shuzan area, but occasionally some are transported from farther afield. "Nothing but live sweetfish," Kunio says firmly. "Dead fish packed in ice taste nothing like live ones."

There are many ways of enjoying sweetfish, including young ones sliced raw as sashimi or as *segoshi* (sashimi with vinegared miso), or preserved in salt. Kunio highly recommends eating them charcoal-grilled with salt, which requires slightly more mature fish. "Sweetfish are a whole food," he says, "like eggs or tomatoes. They're nutritionally balanced. We cook them extremely slowly over a

charcoal fire, so the whole fish is edible, including the head and tail. The skin and the head come out crisp, the flesh is light and delicate, the bones are crunchy and good."

Grilling sweetfish intact may sound easy, but in fact leaving on the head and tail greatly complicates the process. It takes years of experience to produce a grilled sweetfish that's as beautiful as it is tasty. To properly savor a nicely grilled sweetfish, rather than picking it apart delicately with chopsticks Kunio advises a bolder approach: eat every part in order, starting with the head. The aromatic head and skin, delectably sweet flesh, lightly bitter entrails, and flavorful bones add up to a blissful experience that only a whole food can provide.

The most popular way of catching sweetfish is by fishing with a living decoy. A live sweetfish placed on a hook is immersed in water, and when others swim over to defend their territory, they too are caught. At the Katsura River (also known as the Oi River) by Togetsukyo Bridge, anglers can be seen up and down the river every year when sweetfish fishing season opens (usually on the first Saturday or Sunday in June; the season is restricted to protect the species).

On summer nights, fishermen use cormorants to catch sweetfish on the river just outside Kitcho (previous page). The tradition is strongly associated with the Nagara River in Gifu Prefecture, yet it dates back over a thousand years in Arashiyama, too. By the light of pine torches, a black-clad fisherman stands in the helm of his boat, expertly handling multiple cormorants on tethers: it is a picture of summer that perfectly captures the season.

Sightseeing boats called *yakata-bune* allow people to watch the cormorant fishing up close; and Kitcho, too, provides a special pleasure boat for its guests. What could be more enjoyable than *oohing* and *aahing* as the spectacle of cormorant fishing unfolds before you while you feast on delectable Kitcho fare?

THE PLEASURES OF *MITATE*: Crossing Boundaries to Create New Dimensions in Dining

The Japanese word *mitate* means literally to see one thing as another. The principle is applied and enjoyed in myriad ways in Japanese cuisine and in the world of tea, where various unexpected articles are pressed into service as serving or eating utensils. For the technique to succeed, the replacement must lend interest and beauty, crossing boundaries in order to awaken aesthetic awareness. Substitution for its own sake, just as an eccentricity, would be dismissed as vulgar.

An essential part of the tea garden is the stone washbasin (*tsuku-bai*). Before entering the teahouse, guests stoop down to wash their hands and rinse their mouths with its pure water, ridding themselves of the dust of the mundane world. On page 81 is a photograph of the stone basin in front of the teahouse "Yu-an" at Kitcho, its moss-covered, solid appearance conveying a comforting sense of immovable strength. Originally, this stone from the early Nara period (710–94) had a far different purpose: it was designed to support a pillar in an ancient temple. Somehow, over the course of a millennium, its mission as a temple foundation stone came to an end and it took on a key role in the architecture of tea instead.

"Beautiful, isn't it?" says Kunio. "The hollow contains water for purification, so we keep it sparkling clean. But the rest of it goes on getting mossier and mossier, blending in with the surrounding nature. To see something centuries old, recognize its value, and do something new with it comes in part from a sensibility unique to a people raised in an island country, I think. It has to do with the limitations on nature and space. There's a kind of spiritual richness underlying the discovery of this foundation stone and its possibilities."

The photograph in tones of indigo and gray at the right edge of page 50 shows the ground beneath the eaves of the classically designed room named Taikotei. Various materials are used in combination to create a harmony of contrasting colors and forms—an arrangement that serves to catch rainwater that flows from the eaves. The section on the far left, nearest the eaves, is plaster; the wavelike

Salt-Grilled Sweetfish features *ayu,* a prized freshwater fish in Japan, grilled leisurely over coals (above), and then arranged with style and wit in a bamboo basket traditionally used for cormorant fishing.

design beside it is created by roof tiles. But instead of being used on rooftops, the tiles are buried vertically in the ground to form a partition. The freedom of conception is startling. The glistening black stones that hold raindrops are naturally polished Nachiguro pebbles from Mie Prefecture. Standing between the gutter and the garden proper is a line of stones originally cut to serve as pillars, now bordering the coarse white sand of the garden, which is furrowed by the tines of a rake.

"It's got a kind of avant-garde beauty, don't you think?" says Kunio. "Places like this that could just as easily be purely practical and functional are seen as a stage for beauty. It's a peculiarly Japanese sensibility."

Kunio's cuisine, too, overflows with the pleasure of *mitate*, of aesthetic innovation and imagination. The gilded bamboo husk (page 15), orange Chinese lantern pods and green mulberry leaves (page 52), fresh lotus leaves and petals (pages 76–77), and shrimp taro tubers nestled in autumn leaves (page 97)—all are examples of plants used as serving vessels. Even the finely sliced daikon radish that accompanies a sashimi arrangement (pages 20–21) does double duty as garnish and decoration, carefully placed to suggest waves, swirling water, and eddies—the movement of the sea itself. Using natural ingredients such as leaves, flowers, and vegetables in this way gives Kunio's cuisine a distinctive beauty that no porcelain, crystal, or lacquerware dish could ever duplicate.

ABOVE: Kunio exploits a pair of sublimely compatible flavors with *Sea Urchin Grilled in a Kelp Boat*, in which freshly caught sea urchin is cooked in a pouch of kelp over a low charcoal heat, and served topped with kelp.

RIGHT: Another elegant seafood dish, *Abalone Sashimi* again takes advantage of the flavor of kelp, a source of food for abalone. Served with balls of wasabi and abalone liver sauce, radish, and cubes of boiled pumpkin.

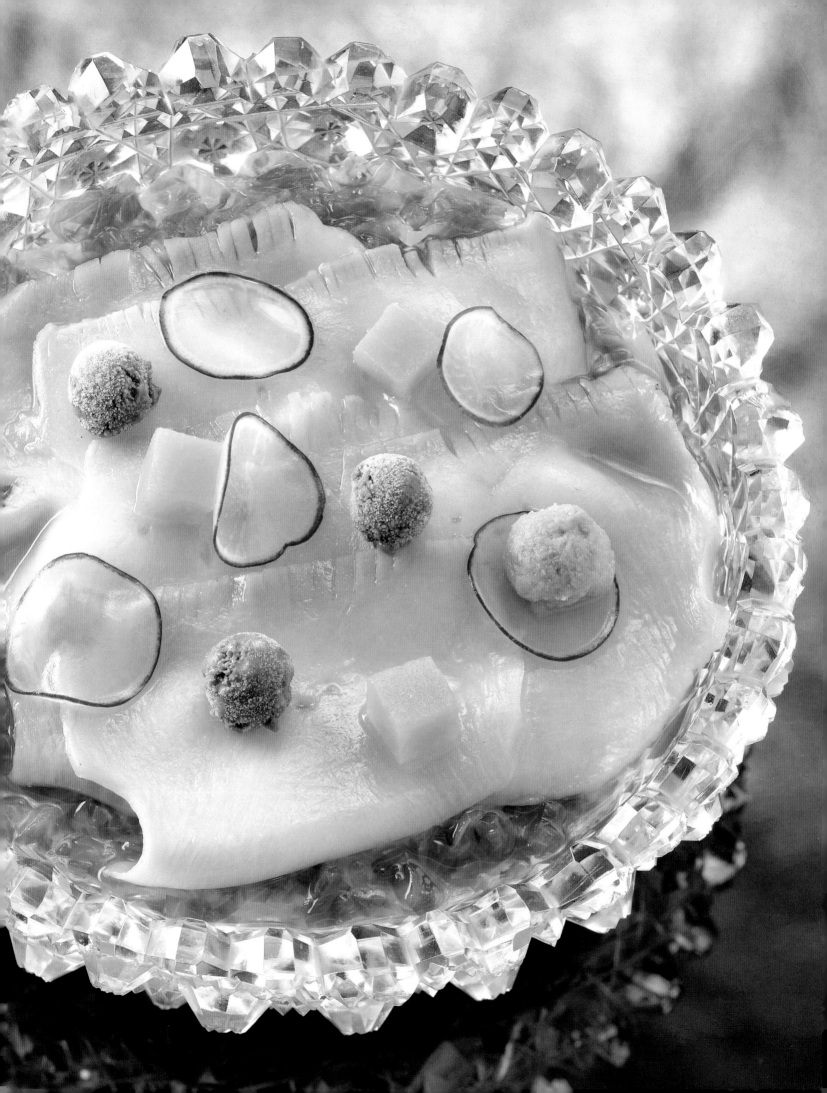

SEA URCHIN AND KELP

Sea Urchin Grilled in a Kelp Boat (page 72) may surprise readers unused to the "heretical" idea of cooking sea urchin (*uni*, in Japanese). True, creamy raw sea urchin has a delicious aroma of the sea, and melts on the tongue with a light, sweet, somewhat briny taste. But the flavor that develops through slow cooking is no less marvelous in its way.

Kunio conceived the idea of cooking sea urchin when he was traveling in Hokkaido and came upon a large stone monument on the beach. Written on the monument was a description of past scenes from everyday life in that region, including an account of children gathering purple sea urchin and horse-dung sea urchin (both Hokkaido varieties) and roasting them over an open fire. Questions raced through Kunio's mind. Foremost among them was: sea urchin comes into season in summer, so why would children make a bonfire at what is, even in the northerly island of Hokkaido, the hottest time of the year? To solve the mystery, he cooked some for himself—and was astonished at how good it tasted.

While roast sea urchin on its own is undoubtedly tasty, introducing a new dish to the Kitcho repertoire requires a more rarefied savor—and so *Sea Urchin Grilled in a Kelp Boat* was born. In scientific terms, the glutamate of the kelp and the inosinate of the sea urchin blend and are transformed, creating a profound new culinary pleasure.

The boat container for the sea urchin is not the only kelp used in this dish. Although unseen in the photograph, bits of the kelp used in making soup stock are inserted between the lobes of sea urchin. In addition, heaped on top is finely chopped kelp.

This lavish use of kelp has a reason: sea urchins feed on it. Break open a sea urchin shell and you will find seawater fragrant with kelp; dark spots are bits of

ABOVE: In *Grilled Abalone Isoyaki*, tender slices of sautéed abalone are laid on a bed of egg tofu and topped with greens and mushrooms before cooking on an individual charcoal burner.

ART: Detail from a hanging picture scroll with a sophisticated design of five overlapping fans, an image evocative of summer. Painted jointly by Sakai Hoitsu (1761–1828) and Tani Buncho (1763–1841).

uneaten kelp. In fact, kelp used to make *dashi* stock sometimes has holes in it left by sea urchins' feedings—a flaw that lowers the value of the seaweed, however fine its quality overall. For kelp harvesters, therefore, sea urchins are an adversary.

For another seafood dish, *Abalone Sashimi* (page 73), the freshest abalone is thinly sliced and then cooked briefly in stock made from primary *dashi* and the flavorful meat around the edge of the abalone. Abalone, too, feed on kelp and other brown seaweed. Like bamboo shoot and young buds of the Japanese prickly ash (*kinome*) or sweetfish and water pepper, the combination of sea urchin or abalone with kelp is another perfect culinary match.

LOTUS

The lotus is native to India, the land of Buddha's birth. It has large, wavy green leaves and a graceful flower of otherworldly beauty, pink and pure white. In the Pure Land of Amida's Western Paradise there is said to be a sacred lotus pond, and in Buddhist statuary, Buddha is often depicted sitting on a "lotus seat" (*renza*)

RIGHT: Another imaginative *hassun* course, *Lotus Flower Hassun, Kitcho Version*, offers shrimp, raw sea urchin, sweet potato, beef tongue, and *hijiki* seaweed in pink petal cups resting on a bed of shaved ice.

In *Lotus Flower Hassun, Kunio Version*, lotus leaves and buds are breezily laced through crushed ice. Fresh sea urchin, grilled abalone, edible chrysanthemum leaves, and bite-sized servings of chicken skin simmered in a sweet sauce and mixed with celery are offered on Baccarat crystal, cool blue porcelain, and lotus leaves and petals.

LEFT: *Sweetfish Rice* showcases one of Japan's favorite local freshwater catches, grilled and filleted, atop rice cooked in sweetfish-laced stock. The whole is sprinkled with a potent Japanese herb called *tade*, minced water pepper, which pairs perfectly with this fish.

RIGHT: *Lotus Rice* combines rice cooked in kelp stock with steamed and sautéed lotus root. This piping hot favorite is topped with dried, lightly salted baby sardines, toasted white sesame seeds, pickled-apricot paste, and slivered perilla leaves, making a fragrant and piquant offering.

BELOW: *Cold Summer Noodles Set in Bamboo* features Japanese *hiyamugi* noodles, garnished with shrimp, shiitake mushroom, and soft-boiled egg yolk. When the bamboo ring is lifted, the noodles merge with the sauce underneath.

in the shape of lotus petals. At the Obon festival for the dead in August, lotus buds are used for decoration, and food offerings to the spirits of the departed are placed on lotus leaves. Local grocers carry the necessary leaves and buds, and most Japanese are deeply familiar with the custom.

Lotus Flower Hassun (page 75), a dish created by Teiichi for the Buddhist Obon festival, continues to be offered at Kitcho to this day. Having learned from his study of tea ceremony that the beauty of nature is integral to kaiseki cuisine, Teiichi incorporated seasonal flowers, leaves, and other natural items into his presentations. This dish in particular shows off his originality, love of nature, and Buddhist sensitivity. When the dish is brought to the table, the lotus leaf is fastened with a cord, concealing what lies inside. When the cord is loosed, the leaf falls open to reveal food of unexpected beauty, putting the diner in the frame of mind of one seated by a lotus pond in the Buddhist Pure Land.

The lotus plant is used widely, not only as a decoration for Buddhist memorial services, but also for sustenance. The young leaves are chopped and steamed with rice or used to make lotus-leaf tea. In Chinese and Korean cooking, glutinous rice is wrapped in lotus leaves and then steamed. The characteristically crisp stem is also edible. *Grilled Summer Vegetables* (page 65) and *Lotus Rice* (previous page) both make use of lotus root. The fruit of the lotus is eaten steamed or grilled, and sometimes candied. Like other Asian peoples, the Japanese excel at inventing ways to use this beautiful and versatile food item.

FLOWERS AND THE SPIRIT OF TEA

Teiichi Yuki had a lifelong love for the tea ceremony that greatly impressed devotees around the country. He hosted an incalculable number of tea ceremonies. Each time, he would painstakingly clean the garden path and stone basin, or *tsukubai*, before preparing a kaiseki meal. He built up a large collection of exquisite tea implements, picking them up one at a time as they struck his fancy, and he loved to linger over them as he made his selection.

Kunio awoke to the significance of the tea ceremony at an early age. "When I joined Kitcho at twenty, I wanted to absorb all I could from my grandfather. To do that, I realized I needed to know the world of tea, and so I told him I wanted to take lessons. That was the beginning."

Based on his grandfather's recommendation, Kunio studied with Soshun Hamamoto, a senior instructor in the Urasenke tradition for whom Teiichi had great respect. Three years later, when he was transferred to the Tokyo branch of Kitcho as an apprentice cook, Kunio continued his study of the tea ceremony, this time following the Omotesenke tradition. Teiichi had frequent occasion to travel to Tokyo, and so Kunio was able to assist him at various important gatherings and tea-related events, gaining an invaluable opportunity to work alongside his grandfather and study his manner and character firsthand. Kunio's exposure to the tea ceremony also strengthened his awareness that Teiichi's vision for Kitcho was anchored in the spirit of tea.

This rustic bamboo-framed window, known as a *shitaji-mado*, is often used in teahouses. To allow light in, one section of a mud-plastered wall is left unfinished, exposing the bamboo lath underneath. The opening is then papered over with handmade *washi* paper. The window pictured here is in Yu-an, the teahouse at Kitcho.

The *tsukubai*, or stone washbasin, is an important feature of any teahouse. This one, located in front of the crawl-through entrance to Yu-an, was originally the pillar stone for a Nara-period (710–94) temple. The same opening that once held a temple pillar is now a receptacle for water.

Kunio created this tasteful, minimalistic arrangement of *miyama renge*, a variety of magnolia, on the verge of blooming. The bamboo vase is by Sen Shoan (1546–1614), the adopted son of tea master Sen no Rikyu.

One early summer day, Kunio was moved to arrange a stalk of budding *miyama renge* (a kind of magnolia; see facing page) in an unpretentious bamboo vase made by Sen Shoan, Sen no Rikyu's adopted son. For the host to provide an arrangement of flowers that reflects his immediate frame of mind is an essential part of tea-ceremony hospitality. Kunio chose buds just on the verge of opening. Visualizing them as growing by a mountain path crowned with morning dewdrops, he scattered water on them. The photograph at left shows the result.

"In my enthusiasm I splashed water all over the wall! I did it to show the beauty and enjoyment to be found in bending the rules of the tea ceremony even as you follow them. That's the spirit I had in mind."

Japanese Shaved Ice with Green Tea Syrup and Bean Jam (below) is based on an old-time summer dessert. Kitcho makes lavish use of the powdered green tea of the tea ceremony, or *matcha*, in this more sophisticated version. The Japanese name for the dish, *Uji-kintoki*, refers to the city of Uji, near Kyoto, which has a long history of growing some of Japan's finest tea. Each spoonful is filled with the grassy aroma and slight bitterness of tea, blending with the sugary bean jam to create a delicate sweetness.

Japanese Shaved Ice with Green Tea Syrup and Bean Jam. Kunio upgrades a traditional summer treat by combining the sweet bean jam with the subtle bitterness of the powdered tea for the tea ceremony (*matcha*) for a refreshing summer dessert. The flavors work wonderfully with the feathery shavings.

FALL KAISEKI

JAPANESE AND THE MOON

The Japanese language has poetic phrases for the beauty of nature, such as *kachofugetsu* ("flowers, birds, wind, moon") and *setsugetsuka* ("snow, moon, flowers"). As such expressions show, the moon looms large in the Japanese appreciation of nature. Perhaps as a legacy of centuries of labor in rice fields, when the lunar phases governed the pace of life, the moon still occupies a special place in people's hearts. Compared to the West, where the full moon is sometimes associated with madness and wolfmen, the Japanese sensibility regarding the moon is rather different.

In the northern hemisphere, the moon shines brightest in September. In Japan the traditional pastime of "moon-viewing" (*otsukimi*), gathering to celebrate and drink in the beauty of the full autumn moon, remains popular. The full harvest moon is particularly revered.

For moon-viewing, people set out sprays of Japanese pampas grass (*susuki*), along with chestnuts, green soybeans, taro root, and other vegetables symbolizing the harvest; there are also special sweet rice dumplings that are white and perfectly round. In the Heian period (794–1185), nobles would go out on pleasure boats and sample choice foods while improvising poems in honor of the moon. Rather than viewing the full moon directly in the sky, they took pleasure in admiring its reflection in a sake cup or on the surface of a pond.

The photograph on page 89 shows a room at Kitcho ready for a moon-viewing party. In the alcove hangs a calligraphy scroll with the single character *tsuki*, "moon." Beneath, an antique insect-cage suggests the season, and arrayed on the veranda are an arrangement of pampas, a pair of high-footed stands heaped with moon-viewing dumplings and assorted autumn vegetables, and a candle stand. Displays of green soybeans and taro root are more typical in other parts of Japan, but Kitcho follows local custom by setting out foods whose names in Japanese contain a repeated "n" sound: *renkon* (lotus root), *ingen* (green bean), *nanban* (corn), *nankin* (pumpkin), *kanran* (cabbage), *ninjin* (carrot), and *ginnan* (ginkgo nut). Such names are considered lucky as they suggest the word for luck, "*un*," the pronunication of the "n" in these words. Kitcho has

RIGHT: The *Moon and Pampas Grass Tray* vividly evokes a sense of autumn, with its "half-moon" tray, wisp of autumn grass, and silver image of a glowing night moon. Tidbits of swimmer crab, okra, egg, and wheat gluten provide a celebration of fall flavors in miniature.

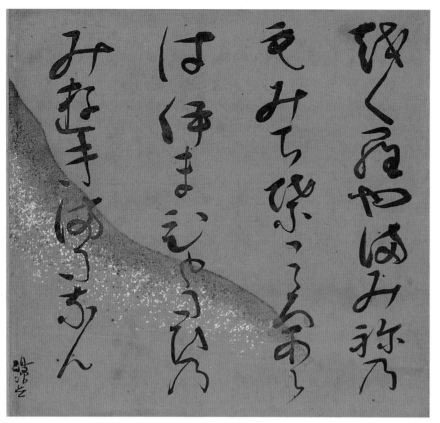

LEFT: Graceful calligraphy by Kobori Enshu on elegant Japanese paper, mounted on a hanging scroll. The name for this room at Kitcho, "Taikotei" (Waiting for the Emperor, shown at right), is derived from this celebrated fall poem. The strip of gold brocade along the left edge of this page is from the scroll mounting.

sweetened the tradition by adding *kanten* (agar-agar), and *anpan* (bean-jam buns), innovations that began in the time of Teiichi's mother.

The room pictured here was added on in 1962, when industrialist Konosuke Matsushita redesigned his villa in Kyoto's Okazaki district and gave Teiichi a building from the garden called a *shoin* (drawing room or study), which was disassembled, transported in pieces to its new home, and rebuilt. The room's transom and other features have been altered, but the distinctive boards of the veranda and the beams of Japanese chestnut oak in the bare timber eaves are original. Teiichi deemed the room fit to display calligraphy (above) by Kobori Enshu (1579–1647), an artist and garden designer who founded his own school of tea and who joins Sen no Rikyu (1522–91) and Furuta Oribe (1544–1615) in the triumvirate of greatest tea masters of all time.

The calligraphy contains this poem by Fujiwara no Tadahira, number twenty-six in the traditional poetry collection *Hyakunin isshu* (One hundred poets, one poem each):

Ogurayama	The maples atop Mount Ogura,
Mine no momiji-ba	Could they but understand,
Kokoro araba	Would keep their brilliant leaves
Ima hitotabi no	Until the emperor of Japan
Miyuki matanamu	Passes this way again.

In the ninth month of 907, when the retired emperor Uda visited the Katsura River, he found the fall colors on Mount Ogura so beautiful that he wished

RIGHT: This classic Japanese room has been readied for an evening of moon-viewing. The calligraphy scroll in the alcove bears the single character *tsuki* ("moon") brushed by Chuho Sou (1760–1838), abbot of the Zen temple Daitoku-ji. The antique insect cage beneath (shown in detail below) is also associated with fall. In the foreground is Kitcho's selection of moon-viewing foods, prepared for a stylish celebration.

Arranged on this specially designed plate is *Sirloin in Special Sauce*. Cubes of premium sirloin, blanketed in a sauce made from red wine, brandy, chicken stock, and beef shank, rest on beds of mashed potato. Equally petite pieces of Kyoto-grown grilled green pepper and steamed and browned sweet potato accompany the steak.

aloud he could show them to his son, the reigning emperor. Chief Minister of State Fujiwara no Tadahira wrote the poem to commemorate the occasion. Mount Ogura is a mountain north of Kitcho; the name once referred generally to the Sagano district, which includes the immediate vicinity of the restaurant.

And so a room in classical *shoin-zukuri* architectural style, fit for an emperor, was added to the restaurant. In honor of Enshu's work, Teiichi named the room "Taikotei," or Waiting for the Emperor Pavilion. This room is always decorated with fine scrolls and art objects in keeping with its illustrious origins.

The moon is also a frequent motif in designs for kimono and eating utensils. The lacquered soup bowls shown on pages 92–93, one of which holds *Shark Fin Turtle Soup*, comprise a set called Autumn Moon Bowls. On the underside of the lids, the new moon, crescent moon, gibbous moon, and full moon are each represented amid trailing clouds. Furthermore, the bowl used for *Sea Bream Chazuke* (page 43) is a copy of Rosanjin's Sun and Moon Bowl, on which gold represents the sun, and silver the moon.

In the Japanese mind, the moon is inextricably associated with rabbits: the dark shadows on the moon's surface take the shape of a pair of rabbits pounding rice, giving rise to the conceit that rabbits live on the moon. Kunio designed this 12-inch plate called Moon Seat (facing page) that playfully reflects this traditional connection.

Kunio has one unforgettable memory of moon-viewing. One year on the night of the harvest moon, he hired a boat to take his guests—accompanied by a geisha—up the river that runs just in front of the restaurant. He prepared a simple meal for the party and served it on board as the boat bore them upstream. Soon the mountains on either side drew in closer, and the river narrowed until they could go no further. Kunio doused the lights and waited with the others for the moon to appear. Mysteriously, although the moon itself remained invisible, they were surrounded by moonlight. Amid a silence so profound that the only other sound was the lapping of water against the hull, graceful notes from the geisha's flute echoed off the slopes and rose high in the sky. Kunio's eyes were drawn to the top of a darkly looming mountain, where he made out the silhouette of an ancient pine, its twisted trunk and branches telling a tale of heroic endurance. Although much slenderer than the iconic pine that is painted as a backdrop on every Noh stage, the tree cast a powerful spell.

"As I stared wide-eyed at that pine, all of a sudden the full moon came sailing out into the sky. I could only tremble at the mystical power of nature."

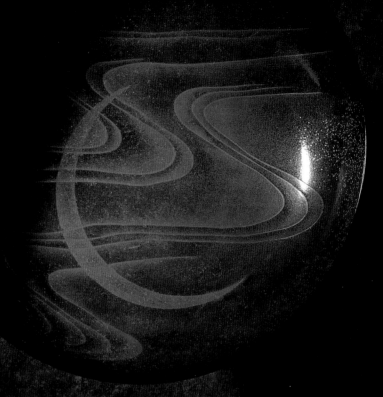

On lifting the black lid of the lacquered soup bowl for *Shark Fin Turtle Soup*, diners get a glimpse of the moon behind wispy clouds. The underside of each lid in the set shows the moon in one of its major phases. Inside, grilled shark fin basks in a turtle broth made in Kunio's inimitable style, seasoned with ginger and garnished with two colors of onion.

SHARK FIN

For centuries, shark fin has been a luxury food item in Asia—especially in China, where its use in high-class cooking goes all the way back to the Ming Dynasty (1368–1644). Japan is among the world's few suppliers of the delicacy. During the Edo period (1600–1868), shark fin was, along with dried sea cucumber and abalone, an important export to China and a main source of income for shogunate coffers. The most highly prized fins are those of the whale shark; the most commonly used, those of the blue shark.

Finning, the practice of harvesting the fins of live sharks and discarding the rest, has lately come under severe fire—but the Japanese have all sorts of appetizing ways of using the entire fish. In the northern prefecture of Aomori, for example, slices of shark meat are blanched, then mixed with vinegar and miso for a delicious treat. In Ise, not too far from Tokyo, white shark fillets are flavored with soy sauce and sweet cooking sake (or simply salted), then dried. Shark meat is also pureed and made into *surimi*, or white fish paste, an ingredient in the popular processed fish cake known as *kamaboko*. Nor does the skin go to waste. The natural roughness of sharkskin makes it an excellent material for wallets and other leather goods. It can even be used as a natural grater—wasabi grated on sharkskin has a distinctively fine consistency and superb flavor.

Sea Bream and Turnip Hot Pot pairs two foods that go beautifully together—the sweet nutty flavor of autumn turnips and meaty white fish. Each is cooked and seasoned separately before being combined in the final soup.

ABOVE: *Kisewata* is an ancient ceremony observed on the occasion of the Chrysanthemum Festival. The colors and style of the flower arrangement are traditional.

RIGHT: Calligraphy from a scroll by a friend of Teiichi's, the renowned Daitoku-ji abbot Daiki Tachibana (1899–2005).

Kitcho's supply of shark fin comes from the city of Kesen-numa in Miyagi Prefecture, which boasts Japan's greatest yearly haul of the fish. Gelatinous and semitransparent, the cooked fin has little intrinsic flavor; its high-end appeal is based rather on its unique texture. Kunio selects especially thick fins for his recipes. In *Shark Fin Turtle Soup* (pages 92–93), he combines the distinctive texture of shark fin with a gourmet flavor. Carefully prepared fins are simmered slowly in chicken stock before receiving one of Kunio's signature touches: for added texture and aroma he grills them on one side, then douses them with the richly savory turtle soup. This enticing dish, of incomparable texture and flavor, is a quintessential example of Kunio's style.

CHRYSANTHEMUM FESTIVAL

The chrysanthemums shown above are arranged in a style associated with the Chrysanthemum Festival, observed on September 9 of the lunar calendar by Japanese courtiers in Heian times (794–1185). People used to lay cotton-like silk floss on chrysanthemums overnight so that it would absorb the flowers' dew

LEFT: Brightly colored fall foliage from persimmon, maple, and zelkova trees is artfully arranged around roasted shrimp taro, so called because of its shrimp-like stripes. The dish itself is appropriately titled *Roast Shrimp Taro amid Fallen Leaves*.

ABOVE: The same traditional Kyoto taro is used in *Shrimp Taro Croquette*, the delicate steamed root accompanied by grilled sword beans, carrot, and shiitake mushroom in a creamy daikon-kelp-onion-butter sauce.

and scent; in the morning they would rub their limbs with the fragrant thread in hopes of enjoying a long and vigorous life. Murasaki Shikibu (978–1016), the author of Japan's supreme masterpiece of prose literature, *The Tale of Genji*, wrote about receiving silk threads for this purpose from Rinshi, who was the wife of Fujiwara no Michinaga (966–1027), the most powerful man of the day. She returned the favor by writing a poem to which she appended this note: "I will touch the threads only briefly, so that you, my lady, may live a thousand years."

The Chrysanthemum Festival was one of a variety of games and feasts held in Heian times, including chrysanthemum-viewing celebrations, chrysanthemum competitions, and poem competitions. Drinking sake with a chrysanthemum floating in it was believed to prolong life. The ancient Chinese valued the chrysanthemum for its medicinal properties, which is why the flower became associated with longevity in Heian Japan and why so many customs grew up around it.

Of the five seasonal celebrations known as *sekku*, celebrated in odd-numbered months, the Chrysanthemum Festival was held to be the most important, as nine is the largest single-digit odd number. In the Edo period (1600–1868), the Tokugawa shogunate prescribed the following days as *sekku:* January 7, Seven Herbs Festival (*nanakusa no sekku*); March 3, the Peach Festival or Doll Festival, a day to celebrate little girls' health and growth (*momo no sekku*; see page 24 for dishes in honor of this day); May 5, the Iris Festival or Boys' Festival, a day to celebrate little boys' health and growth (*shobu no sekku* or *tango no sekku*); July 7, Tanabata Festival, held to pray for progress in traditional arts and crafts; and September 9, the Chrysanthemum Festival (*choyo no sekku*).

At Kitcho, the Chrysanthemum Festival is celebrated by setting out flower arrangements following this rule: the colors of the flowers must be, in descending order, white, purple, yellow, red, and blue. These colors are taken from the ancient Chinese five-elements theory. Arrangements of fresh chrysanthemums are placed only in Kitcho's two most important dining rooms, Taikotei and Fukuroku. Elsewhere, the alcove is decorated with a painting of chrysanthemums or a calligraphy scroll with a reference to chrysanthemums.

Once the most highly regarded of the five *sekku*, today the Chrysanthemum Festival receives scant notice in most households in Japan. But at Kitcho, the old traditions are faithfully followed much as they were in the days of Teiichi, since they resonate on so many levels with both the guests and the food.

Before the *hassun* tray is brought in with its lanterns fashioned from daikon radish, the room lights are dimmed to increase the mystery and beauty of the moment.

Detail of the *Flower-Screen Hassun* tray on the previous page.
A bevy of flowers, food, and glowing "daikon lanterns"
crowds the tray. Among the offerings are shrimp, sea bream,
blue swimmer crab, *gori* fish, and beef tongue.

In *Steamed Yuba Wrap,* another Kunio original, Chinese yam and salt-water eel are surrounded by a layer of *yuba*, or soymilk skin, a delicate Kyoto specialty.

KUNIO AND ROSANJIN

"Sometimes I think I'm the reincarnation of Rosanjin," says Kunio. "I know it sounds strange, but I can't help feeling a strong connection with the man." It's not only that Kunio was born the year after Rosanjin Kitaoji died in 1959. He feels a deep kinship with the twentieth-century giant, a man who left his mark in many diverse fields in Japan, from calligraphy and seal engraving to pottery and cuisine.

Kunio's grandfather Teiichi was also drawn to Rosanjin. Teiichi's book *Kitcho: Teiichi Yuki's Dream* relates the story of their friendship. Around the age of twenty-eight, when after many false starts he finally decided to devote himself to the art of cooking, Teiichi went to Tokyo with the goal of studying at Hoshigaoka Saryo, the restaurant that Rosanjin managed. He cooled his heels in the city for three months, hoping for a chance to work under the celebrated restaurateur, but was forced in the end to return home without even having met him. In later years, after Rosanjin became a frequent visitor to the Kitcho restaurants in Osaka and Kyoto and he and Teiichi were fast friends, Teiichi told him about his ignominious experience.

RIGHT: This refreshing *Persimmon Vinaigrette* mixes pink shrimp, milk-white daikon radish, red carrot, pale orange persimmon, and more in a Tosa vinegar gelée.

What a terrible shame," declared Rosanjin. "I'd like nothing better than to have met you back then. It would have been great fun pitting my experience against your youth."

Rosanjin is famous for his saying, "Dishes are clothing for food," and in fact the connection between serving dishes and cuisine is perhaps closer in Japan than in any other country. Dishes are chosen with an eye not only to the amount of food they will hold, but also to their intended ingredients and presentation. Japanese people often pick up the serving dish and hold it as they eat, so all aspects of a vessel—appearance, texture, size, weight, and more—come into play in the dining experience and influence the enjoyment of a meal.

When choosing antique serving dishes and tea utensils, Teiichi would often seek out Rosanjin's opinion. Rosanjin would place a newly made blue-and-white porcelain dish next to a piece of Ming porcelain and pronounce, "The new one was made by human hands, but the other was made by God. A work of divinity is worth ten times, a hundred times more than anything human, so take good care of it."

How to present cuisine as art? The two men were in agreement that fine cuisine should have dignity, that it should never be treated as a mere background for entertainment. Kunio is heir to this way of thinking, and to the passion his grandfather and Rosanjin both brought to food preparation and the culture of fine cuisine. But beyond that, he feels a bond with Rosanjin's way of thinking—his habit of making judgments based on his own values, free of social norms and ingrained patterns of thinking.

And yet Rosanjin also had this to say: "In making pottery, before you ever handle clay you need to study classic works until you know in your bones what beauty is."

Says Kunio, "I think it was Rosanjin's exhaustive study of traditional Japanese pottery and ancient Chinese pottery that enabled him to discover the standard of value for his own works. That's why despite the passage of time his aesthetic sense still speaks to us, and his name lives on."

Even what seems quixotic owes its presence to a thorough grounding in the classic. Kunio, who learned the living history of Japanese cuisine from his grandfather Teiichi, doesn't seek to rest on his grandfather's laurels but rather to use them as a base from which to determine his own inimitable standard of value. Face to face with works of Rosanjin's that have been handed down to Kitcho (pages 20–21, 39, and 103), he feels this more strongly than ever.

Genji Inkstone Lid Hassun demonstrates another inventive way to display the *hassun* course. It also exemplifies the Japanese aesthetic of *mitate*, where an object's original use is abandoned for a new one (see page 70). Offerings include abalone, fish paste cakes, shiitake, sea bream, and shrimp around a citrus cup of salmon roe.

ORIBE WARE

Oribe ware refers to pottery made in Mino (present-day southern Gifu Prefecture) in the first quarter of the seventeenth century. It's named for Furuta Oribe (1544–1615), a military leader who is revered along with his famed teacher, Sen no Rikyu (1522–91), as one of the greatest tea masters of all time. Some say the name "Oribe" was applied to pottery of the unusual, asymmetrical shapes and designs that Oribe loved; others claim that it referred to vessels whose firing he personally oversaw.

Tea aficionados still delight in bowls of "flawed" or distorted shape, an innovation attributed to Oribe. He was also the first to introduce Christian motifs and other exotic design elements into Japanese pottery. Oribe's aesthetic sense stepped beyond Rikyu's revolutionary beliefs of a quiet, unpretentious beauty. He inherited his teacher's spirit while at the same time opening up a distinctive aesthetic world of his own, one of bold, free conceptions that sparked a rage for "Oribe taste."

One of the most precious examples of Oribe ware at Kitcho is the Oribe Square Bowl with Handle shown on the facing page, in which Kunio has arranged *Yuan-Style Grilled Butterfish* covered with finely chopped citron zest. Teiichi held this vessel in special esteem, and often used it in tea ceremony meals—always to serve grilled butterfish. "Not sea bream, and not tilefish," insists Kunio. "It's funny, but butterfish is what suits this bowl best."

For Kunio, this bowl evokes a particular nostalgia. "It's one my grandfather was fond of and used a lot. When I was twenty, he gave me permission to take it out of its box and wash it. It was a simple gesture that told me he trusted me enough to allow me to handle one of his most valued possessions, and a breakable one at that. Under the pretense of washing it, I was allowed to hold it and examine it. It may not seem like much to some, but I felt really excited and fulfilled. I can never forget it."

This bowl is an example of Narumi Oribe, which uses contrasting red and white clays. The white portion is decorated with a deep copper-green glaze, the red with an inventive line drawing done with white slip under the iron glaze of the lines. The composition's sharp distinction between the deep green and the simple geometric pattern perfectly complements the bold shape characteristic of Oribe ware, achieving a beauty of high sophistication.

"Nice, isn't it? So many different hands have held it through the years, and it's still beautiful, not worn-looking in the least. That's because every generation of owners has loved it and lavished care on it. Above all, the design is so striking; it could easily pass for a new piece. It's astonishing to think this dish is four centuries old. If you tried to make one like it today, you'd never achieve this level of perfection." The work is clearly worthy of its status as an Important Cultural Property. Other examples of Oribe-style ware can be found on pages 102, 103 and 110 (bottom).

Light filtering through the *nijiriguchi*, or "crawl-through entrance," of the teahouse Yu-an.

RIGHT: This antique square Oribe dish holds *Yuan-Style Grilled Butterfish*. The citron zest brings out the full umami of the butterfish, which is marinated before it is grilled.

ABOVE: In this classic presentation of *Kaiseki Hassun*, the offering from the sea is the pearly red specialty *karasumi* or botargo (dried and salt-cured mullet roe), which makes a wonderful accompaniment to sake. The bounty from the land is represented by steamed and grilled water chestnuts.

ART: These fragments from a copy of the ancient Imperial court anthology *Kokin wakashu* are attributed to Ono no Michikaze (894–966). The calligraphy is particularly revered for its artful use of space as well as its graceful brushwork, at once assertive and refined. The square platter incorporates the poems themselves on its surface, and features the design of the purple, gold-embossed cloth used in their mounting top and far-right border of these pages.

KAISEKI'S *HASSUN* COURSE AND THE TEA CEREMONY

On page 53 the meaning of *hassun* was introduced, along with an explanation of the Kitcho style devised by Teiichi and embellished and modernized by Kunio. Now let's consider the significance of the *hassun* course in the tea ceremony. Though the vessel on the facing page isn't the plain, square wooden tray of tradition, it bears a combination of foods appropriate to *hassun*. Kunio has chosen to pair chewy salt-cured mullet roe (*karasumi*) with crisp water chestnuts—a simple harmony of contrasting textures and flavors from sea and land, juxtaposed to symbolize the balance found throughout nature and the universe.

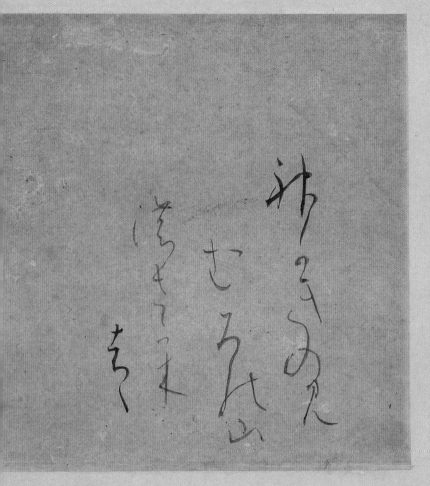

As for Teiichi, he devised a number of other such food combinations for the *hassun* course. In April, for example, he served young sweetfish baked and coated with a salty-sweet miso sauce, paired with broad beans; in September, grilled semi-dried barracuda (*kamasu kazaboshi*) and arrowhead (*kuwai*); in October, flounder fillets (*mushitta konohaga-rei*) and grilled chestnut dumplings; in December, gold sea cucumber and arrowhead. He generally combined two ingredients, occasionally three.

A traditional kaiseki meal served as part of the tea ceremony, or preceding it, begins with a small quantity of cooked rice, served with miso soup and *mukozuke*—an appetizer course consisting generally of raw fish served either as delicate sashimi slices, or mixed with vegetables and seasoned with vinegar, or in a kelp marinade. This is followed by a seafood soup or stew in which broth takes second place to other ingredients. Then comes grilled fish or poultry; extra accompaniments for sake, known as *shii-zakana*; a small bowl of clear soup called *hashiarai*, literally "chopstick rinse"; and finally the *hassun*, followed by a pitcher of hot water with browned rice in it (*yuto*) and seasonal pickles. The *hassun* course thus comes toward the end of the meal.

Kunio describes what happens when the *hassun* course is brought out. "Until the soup course, the host just carries food to the guests, keeping conversation to the minimum. Even though he is reticent, he observes the guests and they him, so wordless communication does take place. But it's during the *hassun* course that he and his guests pour drinks for each other and chat. Everyone shares their impressions of the day's menu and serving vessels, or memories of great meals of the past and whatnot, enjoying the moment. This is when the meaning of the phrase at the heart of the tea ceremony, *ichigo ichi-e*, 'every encounter is once in a lifetime,' comes home to participants."

Before the kaiseki meal takes place, from the time invitations first go out, expectation and excitement build steadily in host and guests, reaching a peak with the *hassun* course. The structure of a kaiseki meal is truly a marvel of perfection.

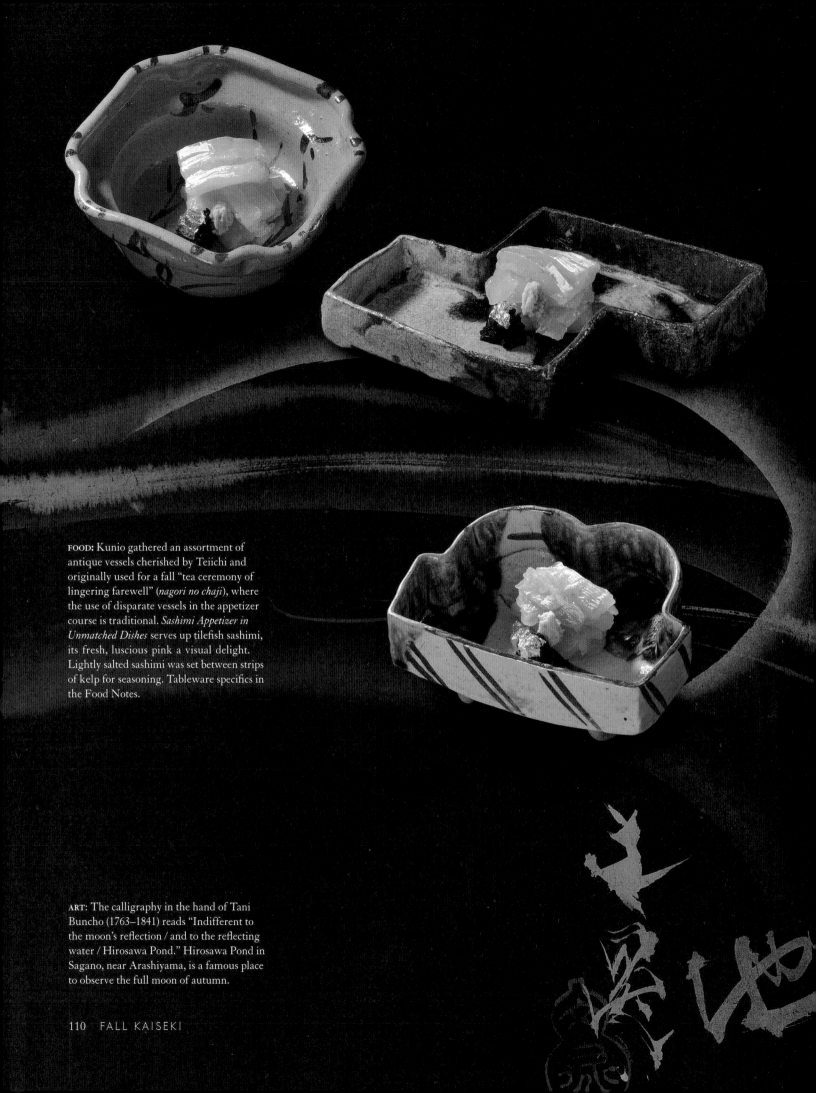

FOOD: Kunio gathered an assortment of antique vessels cherished by Teiichi and originally used for a fall "tea ceremony of lingering farewell" (*nagori no chaji*), where the use of disparate vessels in the appetizer course is traditional. *Sashimi Appetizer in Unmatched Dishes* serves up tilefish sashimi, its fresh, luscious pink a visual delight. Lightly salted sashimi was set between strips of kelp for seasoning. Tableware specifics in the Food Notes.

ART: The calligraphy in the hand of Tani Buncho (1763–1841) reads "Indifferent to the moon's reflection / and to the reflecting water / Hirosawa Pond." Hirosawa Pond in Sagano, near Arashiyama, is a famous place to observe the full moon of autumn.

YOSEMUKO: The Japanese Art of Mixing and Matching

Ordinarily, the appetizer course is served in matching serving dishes, but sometimes each guest receives the same food in a different dish, a practice called *yosemuko* (from *yoseru*, "put together"). This serving style is preferred for the special fall tea ceremony called *nagori no chaji* ("tea ceremony of lingering farewell"), held from the end of October through the beginning of November.

In the world of tea, the new year begins in November, when the "opening of the hearth" (*robiraki*) takes place. This event is celebrated by breaking the seal on the jar containing new tea leaves harvested in the early summer in order to use them for the first time. October, known to tea aficionados as the "month of lingering farewell," marks the end of the year, a time when the old supply of tea leaves dwindles and a sense of sadness prevails.

Fall is, by the nature of things, a time of melancholy and decline, and this year-end tea ceremony brings to the fore aesthetic values of *wabi* and *sabi*—rustic simplicity and the beauty of age and imperfection. As an expression of regret for the passing of the old year, the host uses *yosemuko*, selecting from various oddments: a dish that is the only intact member of a broken set, for example, or a one-of-a-kind piece; dishes that have been patched up because no one had the heart to throw them away when they got chipped or broken. It might seem that such a hodgepodge would have no place at a formal tea ceremony, but using this serving style to express the sadness of parting strikes a chord with tea people and gets at the heart of the sense of beauty encompassed in the ritual. In what might be called an "aesthetic of discord" (*hacho no bi*), grief at what has been lost is expressed by using imperfect remains.

The five vessels pictured on pages 110–111 are all carefully selected gems. Behind the dressings of the *wabi* and *sabi* sensibility, the considerable pleasure of gathering together masterpieces of pottery lies hidden. *Yosemuko* is thus also a way of indulging in the utmost luxury. Of course, it's not enough to assemble a motley collection of fine pieces; their use must express the sadness of farewell while achieving an overall aesthetic balance. If a piece is conspicuously mended, for example, as is often done with beloved ceramics new and old, the patching must be done with charm. Therein lie the enjoyment and difficulty of *yosemuko*.

In these five vessels selected by Teiichi, Kunio has arranged tilefish macerated with kelp, a standard offering, yet one of great distinction. Another challenge of *yosemuko* is arranging the food perfectly in each differently shaped utensil, a test of the server's sensitivity and skill.

"Japanese appreciate arrangements like this, where objects of different types and shapes are mixed together," says Kunio. "The trick is to do it in a way that creates maximum balance and beauty. It's not easy. It takes much more concentration than using matched sets."

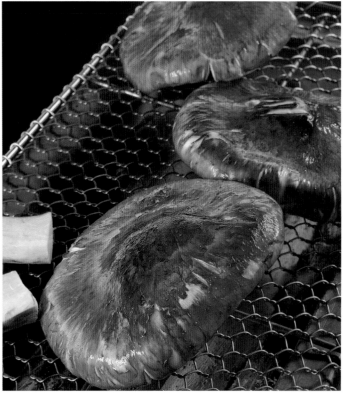

Matsutake Mushrooms Grilled at the Table. The best *matsutake* are as treasured in Japan as truffles are in Europe. To capture the aroma and flavor of this epicurean delight, the mushrooms are grilled in front of the guest by a method involving low, controlled heat and misted paper.

RIGHT: A thank-you note written by the great haiku master and painter Yosa Buson (1716–84) on receiving a large *matsutake* mushroom from his friend and fellow poet-painter Ike no Taiga (1723–76). "Never has there been a specimen so fine—it must be from the village of Yuge in Tamba." He closes by declaring he'll pickle the mushroom to make it last longer, adding this endearing comment: "A pity to eat it, a pity to give it away."

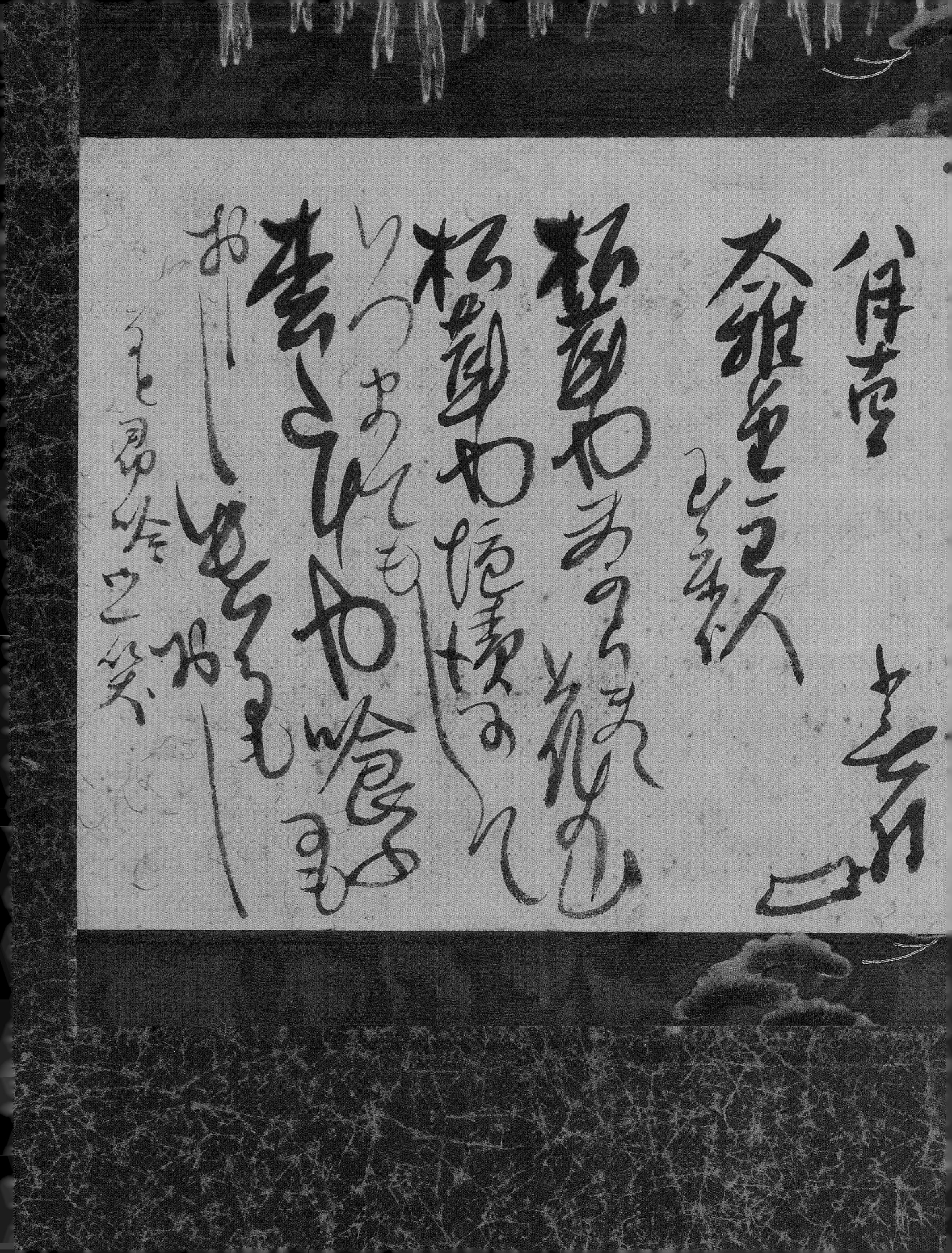

月雪に

松つれもなく煩はす
いつれをも
嵯峨のやまも喰ふ
おもしろくもおもしろ

KING OF MUSHROOMS

As fall deepens, the uniquely pungent aroma of *matsutake* mushrooms (also known as pine mushrooms) penetrates the rooms of Kitcho. Along with foods from the sea, these delectable mushrooms play a starring role in fall cuisine. Kitcho dishes that feature *matsutake* include *Matsutake Mushrooms Grilled at the Table* (page 112), *Pike Conger and Matsutake Mushroom Bowl* (facing page), and *Whole Grilled Tilefish with Matsutake* (page 116), not to mention the classic *Matsutake Rice*.

Grilled *matsutake* is especially fragrant. Concerning mushrooms, the Japanese have an old saying: "For aroma the *matsutake*, for flavor the *shimeji*." Once again taking a contrary position, Kunio begs to differ: "That's what they say, but if you compare fresh-picked samples of each, you'll see *matsutake* gets the nod not just for aroma but for flavor, too."

Bite into *matsutake* and enjoy its satisfying crunch and resilient, meaty texture, followed by a delicate, expanding sweetness. Truly, it is the king of mushrooms.

ART: This superb painting of autumn grasses by Sakai Hoitsu, with his spring painting on pages 36–37, forms two-thirds of a set. The delicate color gradation in the leaves demonstrates his brilliant use of the Rimpa "wet-on-wet" technique.

Pike Conger and Matsutake Mushroom Bowl. For fans of Japanese food, this dish comes close to heaven on earth: it combines two gourmet indulgences, pike conger (page 50) and Japan's most sought-after mushroom.

Conventional wisdom has it that *matsutake* are best before the cap fully opens, while the stem is short and thick. Kunio, however, believes that the key to making the most of this gourmet mushroom lies in matching the shape to the cooking style. He cautions that for maximum flavor, the umbrella cap should be fully opened for grilling, but small and undeveloped for a simmered dish.

Come fall, most Japanese would dearly love to be able to eat their fill of exquisite domestic *matsutake*, but the domestic variety is an extravagance far beyond the reach of ordinary people. It can't be cultivated, and environments favorable to its growth have suffered serious degradation. Many mountainous areas have undergone development, and fewer people can maintain the red pine forests where these choice mushrooms thrive. The harvest has shrunk dramatically since the mid-twentieth century, and today *matsutake* imported from South Korea, China, Canada, and elsewhere far outnumber any local variety.

A dealer from Tamba, a region near Kyoto famous as a source of premium *matsutake*, remembers the old days: "As late as 1960, my shoulder basket used to fill up in no time, and if one or two happened to fall out, well, it was too much trouble to stoop down and pick them up. I'd kick them out of the way and never think twice about it."

TOP LEFT: *Whole Grilled Tilefish with Matsutake*. Salt-marinated tilefish is baked; the *matsutake* are braised and then covered in a thick, *dashi*-based sauce.

TOP RIGHT: *Mushroom Rice*. A cluster of mushrooms—among them Daikoku *shimeji*, *nameko*, and oyster, each type separately prepared to bring out its peak flavor—is set on *dashi*-seasoned rice, then steamed a bit more to finish the dish.

RIGHT: *Crab-Vegetable Mix in Japanese Pumpkin*. Inside a bowl made from a whole steamed pumpkin (*kabocha*) are blue swimmer crab, tofu, shiitake mushroom, pumpkin, carrot, and burdock.

Cut ahead half a century. In the fall of 2009, the price of Tamba *matsutake* was astronomical: well over three thousand dollars per kilogram (2.2 pounds). That any dealer ever kicked a Tamba *matsutake* out of his way is hard to believe.

As a child, Kunio once went to Tamba with his family to hunt for *matsutake*. "They're really hard to find," he says. "They're usually hidden by fallen leaves that blend in with the soil. I don't actually remember, but I'm pretty sure I didn't find any."

The ideal habitat for *matsutake* is in the mountains, in moist soil between the roots of red pines about a foot in diameter. As Kunio learned, fallen leaves tend to accumulate in such crannies on the forest floor, turning to leaf mould and making the mushrooms practically invisible.

Warlord Tokugawa Ieyasu (1543–1616) was particularly fond of *matsutake*, and designated a certain mountain in present-day Gumma Prefecture to provide them for his exclusive use. On their way to Edo, the *matsutake* destined for his consumption received commensurate royal treatment. Their container was marked with a sign identifying the contents with honorific language, and the procession was led by a crier solemnly intoning "Make way for *matsutake*!"

Today, when this traditional but increasingly rare gourmet fare has become a remote dream for most Japanese, such reverential handling may be more fitting than ever.

A STONE LANTERN FOR TWO FAMILIES AND THREE GENERATIONS

The room Taikotei (Waiting for the Emperor Pavilion) looks out onto a garden where the austerity of raked white sand contrasts with lush, deep green moss. A mossy stone lantern lends an aura of serenity and dignity, the effect softened in fall by flowering bush clover. This carefully tended garden, small and unpretentious as it is, transports visitors into a realm of calm. A main reason for the power it exerts is the old stone lantern with its ancient nine-star pattern.

RIGHT: The ancient "nine-star" stone lantern that Teiichi fell in love with at first sight in his youth (see page 121) lends an aura of quiet dignity to the garden in front of the room Taikotei.

Six Fall Desserts. This compartmentalized display of desserts is set in a ceramic plate inspired by a Japanese-style painting palette, once more underscoring the endless possibilities for serving vessel design. Desserts from the upper left, in clockwise order: fig ice cream, steamed chestnut bun, sweetened white bean dough (*nerikiri*) molded into a flower shape, strawberries with jam, chestnut roll cake, and kudzu dumpling flavored with brown sugar.

Originally used as lighting in temples and shrines, stone lanterns were incorporated into the tea ceremony around the time of Sen no Rikyu (1522–91) and began to be used in tea gardens and the gardens of ordinary Japanese as well. Ever since, they have been an important element in the traditional Japanese garden, as indispensable to followers of tea as the stone washbasin.

There's a story behind this lantern, which Teiichi was greatly taken with. "He *loved* this lantern," says Kunio with emphasis. Teiichi first encountered the lantern just prior to World War Two. It belonged to Kasuke Kojima, an antiques dealer in Koraibashi, central Osaka, who had acquired it through a connection with Nara's Akishino-dera temple.

From the beginning, Kojima had taken a strong paternal interest in Kitcho. "Mr. Kojima looked after me," Teiichi wrote appreciatively, "and taught me all about food, art, and business." Two of the most precious possessions in the collection of the Yuki Museum of Art are a Kasuga Shrine mandala (not shown) painted in 1300 and a *tsugi shikishi*—fragments of decorative paper pasted together (pages 108–109)—both Important Cultural Properties that came into Teiichi's possession through Kojima.

Teiichi fell in love with this lantern the first time he saw it, and begged Kojima to let him have it. "He pestered him so much," says Kunio with a grin, "that Kojima, who had no intention of parting with the thing, finally hauled it off to his villa in Saga, Kyoto," to remove it from Teiichi's sight. That villa is none other than the site of Kitcho today. When Kojima passed away quite suddenly after the war, his family put the villa up for sale—and so Teiichi was finally able to gain his heart's desire, purchasing the entire building and grounds for the sake of the lantern.

On the first anniversary of Kojima's death, the Kasuga Shrine mandala was displayed in the alcove at Kojima's place of work in Koraibashi, where Teiichi held a formal tea gathering in Kojima's memory. (Teiichi also purchased that property, the site of the present Koraibashi Kitcho in Osaka.) The stone lantern that meant so much to those two men was passed on to Teiichi's son-in-law Koji and to his grandson, Kunio, who cherishes it, too.

This tea bowl once belonged to the So clan, which governed the small southern island of Tsushima where many Korean potters settled. It therefore became known as Tsushima Ido—"Ido" being a type of Korean pottery. Perhaps the most distinguished piece in the entire Yuki Museum collection, this bowl has a wonderful aura and a beautifully incised foot. Teiichi, who took immense pride in the piece, rechristened it "Kitcho Ido."

WINTER KAISEKI

MAKING WINTER'S GIFTS A PART OF FOOD PRESENTATION

After the capital of Japan moved from Nara to present-day Kyoto, back in the Heian period (794–1185), courtiers made Arashiyama their playground. In spring they went there to enjoy the lovely cherry blossoms, in summer to go boating amid bright greenery, and in fall to enjoy the harvest moon and the brilliant tapestry of red and yellow foliage. The beauty of all of these displays is still appreciated by contemporary Japanese, who come to Arashiyama not just from Kyoto but from all regions of Japan. Indeed, Arashiyama is a popular sightseeing spot for visitors from around the world.

Once the trees in Arashiyama shed all their leaves, a season of austere quiet sets in. The weeping cherry tree in Kitcho's garden, too, stands bare. The only flower in bloom is the small, unobtrusive *wabisuke*, a winter camellia. One's eyes are drawn then to the bright red berries of a small evergreen shrub called nandina or nandin (*nanten*).

"In winter there are fewer people around, and maybe because of the drop in humidity, the air and the sunshine are crystalline," says Kunio. "There's something sad about the time of year, but the sight of red nandina berries and golden kumquats gives the spirits a lift."

The jewel-like berries and kumquats lend color and beauty not only to the landscape, but to winter cuisine as well. Kunio finds them an indispensable ornamental garnish at this somber time of year and uses them often, especially in the showy *hassun* course. Nandina leaves stay green in the winter, so clusters of the berries rival holly as holiday decor. The orange glow of kumquats, too, appears only in the wintertime. It's all the more appreciated as so few spring and summer ingredients are orange in hue.

All sorts of beliefs are associated with nandina. It's said that chopsticks fashioned from it have the power to guard against any poison, while a stout nandina cane will assure long life. In China, where the plant is originally from, people believed that if you used a piece of nandina wood as pillow, you would dream of becoming wealthy.

Golden kumquats tumble from an antique bamboo basket, accented by a bright sprig of nandina berries and offerings of salmon roe and caviar.

The kumquat, a tart and zesty citrus fruit that can be eaten like a grape—rind and all—is also from China. It was introduced to Japan some time around the early fourteenth century. The fruit is a nutritional powerhouse, especially rich in vitamin C.

Kunio says, "The air is dry in winter, and it's easy for people to get colds and sore throats. Kumquat is a traditional remedy for a painful throat, so the Kitcho menu includes kumquats stewed in a sweet syrup. The healing properties of kumquats, their soothing effect on the throat—this is part of folk wisdom built up over centuries of intimate knowledge and experience."

Even in this age of sophisticated science and technology, when the human race can travel to the moon, people still look to folk knowledge to satisfy their perennial desire for a simple, healthy life.

ULTIMATE *TORO* SUSHI

Kunio is the creator and christener of *Ultimate Toro Sushi*. What makes his sushi "ultimate"? Before answering that question, a review of some sushi basics is in order.

Nigiri-zushi (hand-pressed sushi) is one of Japan's most ubiquitous and highly regarded foods. It consists of a hand-molded oblong of lightly seasoned rice streaked with a dab of wasabi (Japanese horseradish)

In order to achieve *Ultimate Toro Sushi*, Kunio creates pockets of air between each grain of rice, rather than pressing it together in the traditional manner. He then slices *toro* sashimi (from the rich belly flesh of the tuna) into three thin layers, which he drapes, one by one, over the rice. The whole creation is built on the tines of a fork to maintain the desired airy lightness.

LEFT: *Arashiyama in Snow*, a hanging scroll by Yokoyama Seiki (1792–1864). Showing snow-laden pines by a bridge against a mountain backdrop, the span in this detail from an antique hanging scroll is immediately identifiable as Togetsukyo Bridge, an Arashiyama symbol. Today, snow softens the contours of the modern concrete structure, recreating the ambience of yore.

and topped with a slice of raw fish or other seafood, or perhaps a bit of omelet. This food comes in endless permutations of size, shape, and ingredients, depending on who makes it and where. In entertainment districts heavily populated with geisha or bar hostesses, for example, a piece of *nigiri-zushi* may be dainty, no bigger than a woman's thumb; while in districts that cater to manual laborers with man-size appetites, it may be eye-poppingly huge. In regions famous for fresh fish or given to lavish hospitality, the topping often dwarfs the rice beneath.

In Kunio's view, "ultimate sushi" must meet three conditions: the rice and the topping must be perfectly balanced in size; both must be exquisitely flavorful; and the rice must be shaped with a touch so light that tiny spaces are left between the grains. His first encounter with the sushi of his dreams took place in a long-established sushi shop in Tokyo.

"An old chef who'd been plying his trade for fifty years or more made me sushi so feathery-light that when he set it on the counter, I could see the rice settle before my eyes. There was air in the bed of rice, so when he put the topping on, the rice sank under its weight. It was masterful. Something you'll never see if the rice is pressed tightly."

Sushi prepared this way doesn't collapse when you pick it up, he adds. "As long as you're carrying it to your mouth it retains its shape, and then crumbles deliciously on the tongue."

To match the old man's bravura performance, Kunio came up with his own idea for "ultimate sushi": instead of shaping the rice in his palms, he would pile it, grain by grain, on a fork. That way there would be tiny spaces between the grains, and even if the sushi was too fragile to hold in the hand, it wouldn't matter. The crowning touch would be the topping—but the usual hefty slice of *sashimi* wouldn't blend smoothly with seasoned rice arranged with such infinite care. Instead, Kunio took an ordinary piece of *toro*, or fatty tuna, sliced it horizontally into three thin layers, and laid them one at a time on top of the rice. This gave the topping enough flexibility to cling smoothly to the moist and tender rice beneath. Transport the finished morsel to the mouth by the fork upon which it is built, and voila! the matchless taste experience of *Ultimate Toro Sushi* with the absolute minimum of compression. A simple yet brilliant idea.

Winter Hassun Course with Nandina Berries. Another stunning *hassun* course, this tray of delicacies is splashed with bright red maple leaves and berries. The course features persimmon with a sesame dressing, mushrooms in a vinegar sauce, boiled arrowhead, simmered shrimp, salt-grilled sea bream wrapped in *nori* seaweed, broiled beef, and vinegared tilefish.

This extreme version of *nigiri-zushi* first came about on a trip to India to provide a catered meal from Kitcho for a certain maharajah. At first, says Kunio, he had planned to use spoons, but switched to forks when he heard that a famous Bollywood actress was to be among the guests. "Spoons are pretty wide in diameter, and I assumed she wouldn't want to open her mouth wide in front of other people."

In his tireless quest for perfection, Kunio is willing to go to mind-boggling lengths for improved flavor. His approach to making the vinegared rice used in sushi is a prime example. Cookbooks advise, "Fold the rice with a wooden spatula, using swift, horizontal slicing motions." Circular stirring motions might damage the tender grains, but making slicing motions with a wooden spatula cannot ensure that each grain will be coated with vinegar. To solve the problem, Kunio adds vinegar while picking apart the freshly steamed rice with chopsticks, grain by grain.

Nigiri-zushi originated and flourished in Edo (now Tokyo) some two hundred years ago. Until then, the word "sushi" referred to *nare-zushi*, an ancient method of preserving fish by combining it with rice and leaving it to ferment naturally over a period of months. This method was in use as early as the Nara period (710–94). As time passed, variations were introduced to shorten the waiting time, until in the early nineteenth century the pickling was dropped entirely and fresh raw fish was served on freshly cooked vinegared rice. At first, like soba noodles and tempura, *nigiri-zushi* was served from stalls as a snack— the Edo version of fast food. It makes sense that the highly spirited Edokko, as inhabitants of the city were known, would appreciate a food at once tasty and handy, ready to be enjoyed at any time without fuss or waiting.

WINTER SEAFOOD AT KITCHO: Pacific Snow Crab, Blowfish, Himi Yellowtail

Varieties of winter seafood that thrive in the cold, stormy waters along the coast of the Sea of Japan include Pacific snow crab (*zuwai-gani*), blowfish or puffer fish (*fugu*), and yellowtail (*buri*). The snow crab is prized for its sweet and silky flesh; the blowfish for its distinctive, elegant flavor, which increases in umami as you chew; and the rich yellowtail for its buttery goodness and clear, sweet aftertaste. All three are luxury fare, and at Kitcho, they are quite simply the best of the best. Guests are treated to each of these epicurean delights at their pinnacle.

The Japanese name for snow crab varies depending on where it's caught. In San'in (an area along the coast of western Japan) it's called *matsuba-gani*, in northern Niigata, *echizen-gani*. Most popular of all is *taiza-gani* from the Tango Peninsula in northern Kyoto Prefecture, near the Sea of Japan. In the photo of live crabs on page 132, the one in the middle has a green band visible around one claw (in fact, all three crabs are thus marked). This designates a *taiza-gani*. With only five fishing boats in operation, the local catch is extremely low, and the *taiza-gani* is an almost impossibly rare find—one that's prized not for its scarcity but for its superb quality.

The delicate scent of incense greets every Kitcho guest. Classic incense trays like this are common accessories for the tea ceremony, and in years past were used when smoking a *kiseru*, the long, thin tobacco pipe of old Japan.

RIGHT: *Crab and Butterbur Buds Simmered in White Miso.* Hot crab cooked at the table in a mellow white miso seasoned with *dashi* is an irresistible winter treat.

"The boats that go after *taiza-gani* are small," says Kunio. "Too small to catch very much of anything at one time. They always go out and come back the same day. As soon as they're back in harbor, the men boil up their crab catch. The meat is so fresh, it tastes out of this world."

Larger fishing vessels stay out at sea at least overnight, and sometimes as long as four or five days, keeping their catch alive in tanks till they return. But crabs are sensitive creatures; they start wasting away the moment they're caught, so their meat quickly diminishes in substance and flavor. The key to ensuring maximum flavor is to boil them within hours. Any live crab is bound to taste good, but the lusciousness of crabs brought straight back and plunged into boiling water, as the *taiza-gani* are, is beyond compare.

Not that boiling them just any old way will do. When he orders *taiza-gani*, Kunio always asks for ones from the third boiling. The crabs are thrown into huge vats of boiling, salted water, several at a time. "The ones boiled first acquire only the flavor of salt from the broth. By the third batch, the umami of the first and second batches has permeated the broth, and it tastes just right. By the fourth or fifth go-round, the broth is too concentrated, overwhelming the essential delicacy of crab." Kunio's determination to provide the finest food possible is reflected in such scrupulous attention to detail.

Every region has its own characteristic ways of boiling crabs, he adds. The flavor of crabmeat is influenced by factors such as how many crabs are cooked together at one time, for how long, and how often the cooking broth is changed; this explains why San'in crabs are mild in flavor, those from Echizen more intense.

A green leg tag identifies *taiza-gani*, a kind of Pacific snow crab prized for its outstanding freshness and flavor.

RIGHT: In winter, piping hot dishes revive the body and stave off the season's chill. For *Pacific Snow Crab Hot Pot*, tender crab meets succulent Chinese cabbage in a seasoned *dashi* stock. The dish is simple, hearty, and mouthwatering.

Flavor also depends on the crab's place of origin and individual features, as well as when it was caught and how it was boiled. Before he cooks with crab, Kunio takes all these elements into account to select the best method of preparation.

■ ■ ■

There are some two hundred varieties of blowfish, or *fugu*, but only a handful of them are edible. The most famous include *tora fugu*, *ma fugu*, and *akame fugu*. Of these, *tora fugu* is valued the most, and this is of course the variety used at Kitcho.

Japanese fondness for blowfish (also known as puffer fish or globefish) goes all the way back to the Stone Age: its bones are found in great quantities in shell mounds across the country. *Fugu* is known also for its deadly toxin. Though some varieties are harmless, the internal organs of most *fugu* contain lethal amounts of tetrodotoxin, a poison so virulent that even a tiny amount can cause paralysis or death. There is no known antidote. An old saying goes, "I want to eat *fugu* but I don't want to die." And the venerable haiku master Basho once penned this haiku, in evident relief: "Nothing has happened! / One full day has now gone by / since I dined on *fugu*." Back before the locus of the danger had been scientifically pinpointed and a system of licensing put in place for *fugu* chefs, accidents must have been commonplace. With black humor, Osakans traditionally refer to the fish as *teppo* or "pistol," a nod to its inherent risk.

Although the risk is common knowledge, devotees of *fugu* cuisine are legion. The flesh has almost no fat and a very light flavor; its place in Japan's culinary pantheon is assured by a deep, complex umami that emerges gradually as it is chewed. Today, protected by various safeguards, diners can relax and focus on this delightful taste sensation.

Blowfish is eaten in a variety of ways: in hot pots, fried, grilled, or thinly sliced as sashimi. Kunio is especially particular about the latter, stressing that the slices should not be paper-thin. "Thin, yes, but still satisfying to bite into. It's important to slice them to just the right degree of thinness for optimal consistency and texture."

■ ■ ■

Kitcho uses wild yellowtail (*buri*) from Himi fishing port, which lies on a continental shelf in Toyama Bay, Toyama Prefecture. The area is especially renowned for its *kamburi*, or winter yellowtail, far and away the finest to be had. Kunio is lavish in his praise: "The winter yellowtail from Himi is rich in fat and melts in your mouth, but leaves no aftertaste. The aroma is wonderful, too. It's really delicious."

Kunio prepares different parts of the fish differently. For example, the succulent, rich belly is tasty as it is, so he uses that for sashimi; the meat along the back he grills for extra flavor.

Throughout Japan, the yellowtail is known by different names at different stages of its life, with regional variations. In Kanto, for example, the names

The winter-blooming camellia has long been a seasonal bright spot for the Japanese, especially among tea practitioners. It appears at Kitcho in the garden and in flower arrangements.

RIGHT: In *Crab and Grilled Tofu Soup*, crab meat is steamed until tender, then shaped and set on a square of hot tofu. Blended into the seasoned soup are creamy crab innards (*kani miso*), a prized delicacy in Japan.

are *wakashi*, *inada*, *warasa*; and in Kansai, *tsubasu*, *hamachi*, *mejiro*. Because such name changes suggest a steady sequence of promotions, the yellowtail is also known as *shusse uo*, or "fish of success." In Toyama and neighboring Ishikawa prefectures, it's customary to send a year-end gift of yellowtail to the family one's daughter has married into, thereby extending wishes for prosperity and success. The *hamachi* widely sold in Japanese supermarkets, incidentally, is a cultivated variety of yellowtail.

YOBANASHI: Tea for a Winter's Night

Winter is a time when we slow down and become introspective, and *yobanashi* ("evening conversation"), a formal tea ceremony that begins at dusk in winter,

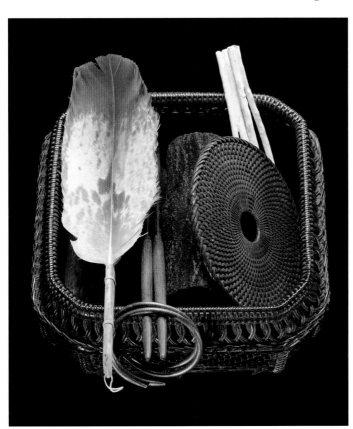

A charcoal container (*sumitori*) holding equipment needed to renew the fire in the sunken hearth: a feather brush, tongs, iron rings to lift the kettle, a large round piece of charcoal, charcoal made from tree twigs and painted with white lime, and a rattan kettle rest.

is the perfect way to satisfy that inclination. One of the seven main styles of *chaji* (the serving of formal tea with a full meal), *yobanashi* is intended as a chance for guests to while away the long, cold night through relaxed, intimate conversation with the host and with each other. The garden path is lit by lanterns or candles, and a bucket of warm water is set beside the stone washbasin to mitigate the chill of icy water as guests purify themselves before entering the tearoom.

The seven modes of formal tea are divided according to the time of day and other conditions. They consist of *shogo no chaji* (noon tea), *asa chaji* (morning tea), *yobanashi no chaji* ("evening conversation" tea), *akatsuki no chaji* (dawn tea), *hango no chaji* (tea with light meal and Japanese confections), *atomi no chaji* ("follow-up" tea, served at the request of nonattendants to view art), and *fuji no chaji* ("irregular" tea, a more casual tea for unexpected guests). The most representative of these is noon tea. In addition to these basic seven, there are a number of other styles, among them *kuchikiri no chaji*, a tea ceremony celebrating the breaking of the seal on a jar of new tea, held in November; *nagori no chaji*, a tea ceremony honoring the last of the year's supply of tea and seeing out the warmer months before winter sets in, held in October; *ikkyaku ittei no chaji*, a tea ceremony with one host and one guest only; and *torai no chaji*, a tea ceremony in honor of someone who has presented a tea utensil to the host.

The photograph on the facing page shows Yu-an, the tearoom at Kitcho, ready for a *yobanashi* tea. The room is lit only by the glow of a candle, burning embers in the hearth, and a lamp (unseen). The slightest movement of host or guests—their very breathing—makes the flame waver, sending flickers of light into dark corners so that shapes there rise up dimly, while what lay faintly visible close at hand is swallowed in darkness. The constant interplay of light and shadow is simply beautiful.

Teiichi once wrote, "Experiencing a *yobanashi* tea ceremony impresses on you the softness of firelight inside a tearoom." Kunio, too, has several unforgettable memories of *yobanashi* tea ceremonies. One of them is an episode from his

Chewy, sweet, and visually elegant when thinly sliced, *Translucent Blowfish Sashimi* features another prized element of Japanese cuisine. Kunio places a heap of grilled skin at the center of the dish, highlighting an often-neglected piquancy.

youth, when as a young man in his twenties he was invited to his first *yobanashi* occasion. All the other attendees were elderly tea masters and connoisseurs.

"During the meal, they kept pressing sake on me, urging me to drink up because I was young," he recalls with embarrassment. "The dim light and the murmur of water boiling in the teakettle, which is often likened to the sound of the wind whispering in pine trees, were so soothing that before I knew it, I drifted off." He drank the offered sake with enjoyment and then, with equal enjoyment, went to sleep. Such behavior is the privilege of youth—or better, a mark of Kunio's unpretentious charm. It's easy to imagine the others smiling indulgently at the sight of him succumbing to drowsiness.

Kunio also vividly remembers being around thirty when, at his grandfather's urging, he hosted his first *yobanashi*. He did the preparations himself, readying the garden and stone washbasin, cleaning the tearoom, assembling the utensils, planning the menu, and preparing the tea—all unassisted for the first time. Only in the preparation of the food did he have the help of a young cook.

"When my grandfather hosted a tea ceremony, he would unhesitatingly use the finest utensils, the sort that are housed now in the Yuki Museum," recalls Kunio. "We had nothing at Kitcho to equal his collection, but I was determined to come as close to his level as I could." The expression he uses to convey his determination, *kokoro o kudaku*, translates literally as "pulverize the heart"; it is the same expression used by Zeami (1363–1443), the famous aesthetician and playwright, to describe the attitude required of a Noh actor assuming a role. That is the level of commitment that lies at the heart of tea.

"In the dim interior of the tearoom at a nighttime tea ceremony, your awareness becomes highly focused. Your heart turns inward to confront itself and at the same time reaches out to others, making possible the exchange of unseen emotions. This is the goal of every tea ceremony, but at a *yobanashi* ceremony, the mingling of firelight and darkness creates a special atmosphere of even greater intimacy."

To see into one's own heart and the hearts of others: this is Kunio's interpretation of the meaning of the *yobanashi* tea ceremony, deepened by his own experience as host.

ABOVE: *Battledore Hassun*. The tray, in the shape of a paddle used for a traditional New Year's game, offers up mullet roe, shrimp, arrowhead, sea bream, and black beans in gelatin. The lidded containers hold herring roe, caramelized anchovies, and sea cucumber innards.

CENTER: A detail from the mounting of the celebratory hanging scroll *Fukujuso* (Adonis flower), shown in the alcove on page 146 and in detail on page 157.

元日浴あまりて月のある如く

FOOD: *Yellowtail Teriyaki with Egg-and-Yam Sauce.* Fatty and rich in winter, yellowtail is here basted with a soy sauce-*mirin* combination and served with a sauce made from primary *dashi* stock, egg yolk, and Chinese yam. The dark green condiment is chopped carrot shoot, which has a peppery mustard flavor.

ART: The calligraphy on a ground of red is from a hanging scroll with a New Year's poem by Kitamura Kigin (1624–1705), haiku teacher of the great Matsuo Basho.

The magical effects wrought by firelight and darkness are not limited to the realm of tea, of course. Kunio recalls experiencing something similar at a riverside barbecue with friends, as they sat in twos and threes at dusk. Slowly the mountains in the distance and the river in the foreground changed from subdued gray to black. As the party gazed into the light of candles they'd brought along, their voices died away and the quiet deepened. Kunio remembers that everyone's gaze turned inward, and people were moved to honesty. One by one his friends shared reminiscences tinged with self-examination, their stories finding echoes in their listeners' hearts.

"That's the same as *yobanashi*," says Kunio. "There's something about the combination of darkness and natural lighting that inspires meditation and confidences, takes people to an essential plane and strengthens their connections." He adds thoughtfully, "The reason the tea ceremony has lasted down the centuries must be that it was a necessary way for people to form bonds."

■ ■ ■

The teahouse at Kitcho, Yu-an, was a gift to Teiichi from his children in 1989, on the occasion of his eighty-eighth birthday. He expressed his joy in a special commemorative mode of tea ceremony that he hosted twenty-five times over the next six months. Among the utensils he used on these occasions were the calligraphy by Sen no Rikyu shown on page 150 and the tea scoop carved by Rikyu shown on page 151.

The teahouse contains two small rooms, each holding four and a half tatami mats. One is in *doan* style, where the host's mat and the guests' mats are separated by a middle post and a wall with an opening that has an arched top. The other is in *shoin* style, with an alcove (*tokonoma*) for the display of flowers and art objects and staggered shelves built into the wall (*chigai-dana*). The rustic window on page 80 is from the *doan* room; the composition of the bamboo lath is said to show Teiichi's fine aesthetic sensibility and attention to detail.

To this day, Yu-an is used for all types of tea ceremonies.

CELEBRATING THE JAPANESE NEW YEAR AT KITCHO

As the old year draws to a close, households across Japan put up gala New Year's decorations that reflect people's hopes for a happy new year. The same is true at Kitcho, where the festive decorations have an air of antique elegance.

At either side of the front gate are *kadomatsu*, or "gate pines," one male (*omatsu*) and one female (*mematsu*); following Kyoto tradition, these are small pines with their roots attached. Under the eaves at the entrance is a decoration made of a sacred rope of braided straw (*shimenawa*), bitter orange (*daidai*), a kind of rhododendron called *yuzuriha*, and *urajiro* fern. Like the gate pines, these are displayed to mark the way in for the *toshigami*, the deity of the incoming year.

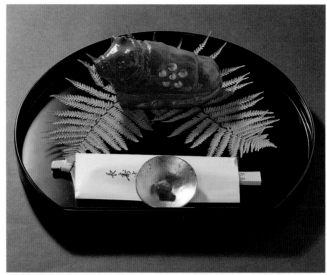

ABOVE: This *New Year Appetizer Tray* calls for a food vessel in the likeness of the animal that rules the coming year—the *toshitoku*, or "year-luck" deity. Removing the lid of this ox-shaped vessel reveals traditional New Year's delicacies: dried caramelized anchovies, herring roe, and salted mullet roe with sliced radish. The pheasant morsels in the gold sake cup will be doused in hot sake to create "pheasant rice wine," a New Year's treat well and truly fit for an emperor.

RIGHT: New Year's decorations in the Fuku-roku room. Manifesting a wish for eternal happiness, a garland of traditional *musubi-yanagi*, or "tied willow," spills to the floor and trails across the alcove in lavish Kitcho style. Long willow branches just on the verge of budding are bound together in a generous ring, the roots ensconced in a bamboo vase along with an arrangement of red and white camellia. The scroll painting is *Sunrise* by Tosa Mitsuzane (1780–1852), paired with a traditional New Year's decoration. The lobster's curved back suggests old age, and hence longevity.

On the right as you step inside is a hanging scroll by Rimpa painter Sakai Hoitsu (1761–1828), inscribed with a celebratory haiku for the New Year: "Here in our lodging / first laughter of the year / *fukujuso*" (page 146, detail on page 157). Because it blossoms around New Year's Day (by the old lunar calendar), *fukujuso* (Adonis plant) is considered auspicious; its name means literally "happiness-forever-grass." To the left of the scroll is a substantial floor-length garland of hanging coral evergreen. On display in the alcove of each of the seven private rooms is an item traditionally associated with good luck: *musubi-yanagi* (tied willow), or an object in the shape of a Chinese zodiac animal, or straw rice bags overflowing with good-luck charms. Furthermore, the faded bamboo used in the garden well lid, troughs, and gate is exchanged for fresh green bamboo.

"The New Year's decorations we use today are the tangible form of prayers for happiness by Japanese people of old," says Kunio. "In that spirit, we do all we can to fashion them by hand."

To make the distinctive floor-length decoration, for example, the kitchen staff harvest coral evergreen (*hikage no kazura*) from a special place in the mountains where it grows wild, and arrange it by hand. As the photograph shows, the splendid garland is long enough to spill onto the *tatami* mats. The swath of "tied willow" displayed in the *tokonoma* alcove (previous page), too, is handmade by Kitcho staff. It must surely be the longest, most luxurious example in all Japan.

Rooted plants, plants of unusual length, and circular plants: items like these are displayed at New Year's for a reason, of course. They represent the hope that the family may put down solid roots and flourish for generations to come, as well as prayers for long life and eternal bliss.

Coral evergreen is considered auspicious because it stays green for a long time, as the name implies, and spreads wide and far across the ground. It also plays a part in an episode from the dawn of Japanese history. As the tale goes, the sun divinity Amaterasu (said to be the founder of the Imperial house) grew angry at the rampaging of her

Kasujiru. Kasu are sake lees, left over from brewing. When used in cooking or soup, as here, they bring a hearty taste to foods. Filling out the soup are chicken, daikon radish, carrot, shiitake mushroom, shrimp taro (*ebi-imo*), and finely minced citron.

brother the storm god, Susano-o, and shut herself away in a rock cave, plunging the world into darkness. After holding a council to devise a way to entice her out again, the gods threw a party in front of her cave, according to a famous passage in the *Kojiki* (Record of Ancient Things, 712 A.D.). Ame-no-uzume, the goddess of the dawn and laughter, performed a nude dance to loud applause, covering herself with the leaves of the coral evergreen. When Amaterasu, her curiosity roused by the noise, pushed aside the rock slightly for a peek, she was hauled out, and light and peace were restored to the world. Because of its association with this story, coral evergreen is often used in Shinto rituals, and was incorporated in dancers' headdresses in ancient times.

Sirloin Sashimi Seasoned with Kelp. In Japan, sashimi is no longer limited to seafood. Beef liver, chicken, and other meats are also served in this style; they need only be incomparably fresh. The sirloin is seasoned lightly with salt and kelp stock, and served with dabs of mashed potato, Japanese mustard, ground chili peppers, chives, and crisped rice.

With all its New Year's decorations in place, Kitcho seems even more sparkling and fresh than usual. Guests are bound to be cheered, sensing that the coming year is filled with promise. Perhaps they will even decide to decorate their homes in a similar style.

"We do it this way because it's part of our mission as a restaurant to transmit Japan's traditional culture," says Kunio. "But actually, I don't think it really matters what you do or don't put on display for New Year's. All that matters is that you show sincerity."

The New Year's food served in these pure and spotless surroundings is, of course, utterly extraordinary. The vessels and food alike are carefully chosen to incorporate as many items associated with good fortune as possible. The three "musts" for any New Year's menu are herring roe (*kazunoko*), suggesting the blessing of many children; dried anchovies caramelized with soy and sugar (*gomame*), which suggest a rich harvest; and sweet black beans (*kuromame*), associated with working hard (termed *mamemameshiku* in Japanese). At Kitcho, in addition to herring roe it is customary to serve botargo (dried, salted mullet roe), another superlative delicacy, which the staff begins to make as early as October.

ABOVE: A gold sake decanter and cups are decorated with pine, bamboo, and plum, a good-luck trio representing constancy, resilience, and vitality.

AN APPETITE FOR INNOVATION

The first modern chef to include beef in a full-course Japanese-style meal was probably Teiichi, who didn't limit himself to traditional ingredients but happily made use of caviar, foie gras, and any other international delicacies he discovered. His grandson Kunio firmly embraces this inclusive approach to cooking as well.

"The greater ease of distribution today, and the speed with which we can now gain information about specialized foods, create a strong sense that the world has shrunk drastically," says Kunio. "Given that times have changed, how can we cooks go on doing everything exactly the same as in the past? I think

FAR LEFT: This entryway décor, at once pure and sublime, shows Kitcho's take on ancient New Year's customs. The eye-catching floor-length decoration on the left is made from an abundance of coral evergreen.

Flower Petal Rice Dumpling Bowl is named after a
confection commonly served at the first tea ceremony
of the new year. The traditional filling for this confection is *miso-an*, miso-flavored bean jam, but this one
has *ebi-shinjo*, a kind of shrimp paste, at its center.

ABOVE: *Eggs Kunio* combines delightful soft-boiled "hot-spring eggs" with roast beef and shiitake mushrooms, infused with the chef's trademark sauce (see *Sirloin in Special Sauce*, page 180).

LEFT: *Low-Temperature Sukiyaki* uses Kunio's special sauce and a golden-hued sauce made from egg yolk and chicken stock to reinvent this old Japanese classic.

traditional cuisine—including the regional cuisines that still exist all around Japan—must be rebuilt from the bottom up."

Kunio is adventuresome in incorporating not only ingredients but also culinary techniques from overseas into his cooking. One good example is his version of sukiyaki, a dish that, for many foreigners, is virtually synonymous with Japanese cuisine.

Generally speaking, there are two ways of making sukiyaki: the Kanto way and the Kansai way. In terms of food culture, Kanto could be defined very broadly as Tokyo style, Kansai as Kyoto-Osaka style. In Kansai, a cube of beef lard is melted in a heated pan; the meat is then browned and seasoned directly with a mixture of sugar and soy sauce. After that, long onion, shiitake mushrooms, Chinese cabbage, and other leafy vegetables are added to the pot and simmered in the broth, which is replenished as needed with additional soy sauce, sugar, and water. In Kanto, on the other hand, the first step in making sukiyaki is to prepare the sauce, a mixture of *dashi* stock, soy sauce, sugar, sweet cooking sake (*mirin*), and other flavorings. After the sauce is brought to a simmer in the pan, the meat and vegetables are added. In both Kansai and Kanto, the cooked ingredients are dipped into beaten raw egg before eating. This cools the hot ingredients, adding substance to the flavor.

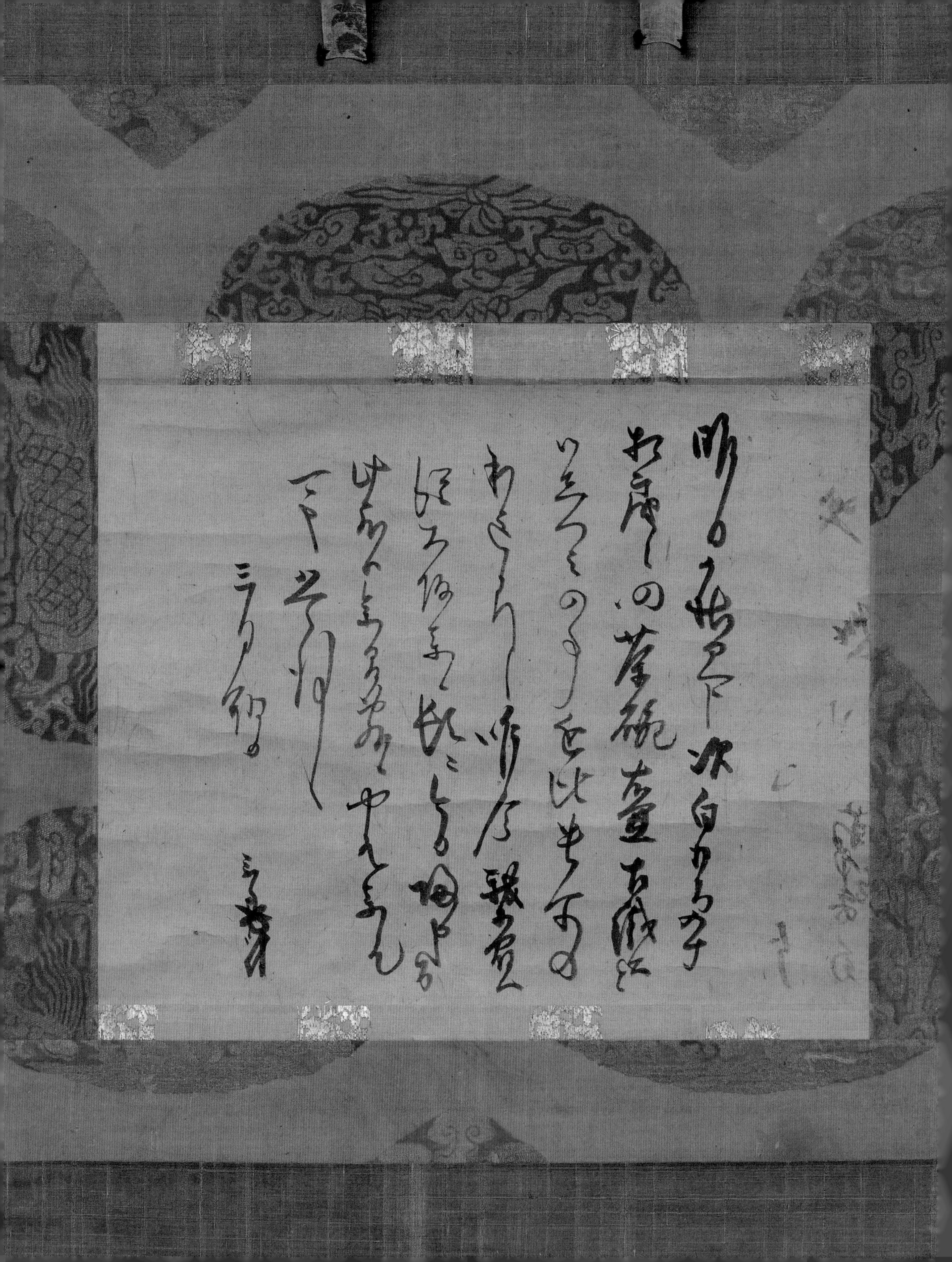

明くる年下れば白からず
野辺の若菜をつみてこそ
わきてのみをひきもする
ひきしのひしに
せきもせきぬ中にまし
下そ用し
三月初

The focus of Kunio's sukiyaki is on top-quality beef. To add complexity and subtlety to the taste, he introduces truffles and the popular Italian salad green, arugula. For seasoning, he uses his own sauce, and in place of a beaten raw egg he substitutes his signature custard sauce (see page 184). One other point: he heats the first sauce to exactly 150 °F (65 °C). Extensive experimentation has convinced him that simmering beef at this temperature brings out its flavor best.

Sukiyaki is a relatively recent addition to Japanese cookery, a Meiji-era innovation made under the influence of Western culinary styles. Prior to the Meiji period (1868–1912), most average Japanese had never even seen beef. Once they grew familiar with steak, beef stew, and other such dishes, however, they adapted them to their own liking, and sukiyaki was one result. Kunio went back to the basics of this iconic dish, considered the aspects of ingredients and cooking method separately, and reconfigured each one in a more European manner through his own sensibilities. In so doing, he put his own stamp on sukiyaki, creating a new, delicious version à la Kunio.

Sirloin Sashimi Seasoned with Kelp (page 145) also brings out the rich flavor of beef to the fullest extent. The technique used here is usually reserved for sliced raw fish such as tilefish, flounder, sea bream, or other white-fleshed fish. Each slice is wrapped in kelp, which imbues it with a subtle, complementary flavor. The dry kelp slowly draws moisture out of the raw fish while steadily changing its texture. At the same time, the inosinate in the fish merges with the glutamate in the kelp, redoubling the umami flavor. Kunio has applied the same principle to beef, repeatedly brushing thin slices of raw beef with kelp stock. Here, too, the kelp flavor collides and merges beautifully with the inner fibers of the meat, creating a supernova of flavor.

Lately Japanese have taken to Western-style steak tartare and Korean-style carpaccio (J: *yukke*, K: *yuk-hoe*), but eating raw fish is still far more common. Popularity notwithstanding, Kunio's kelp-wrapped version finds a warm welcome among Japanese, who love any umami-rich food. Kunio's many innovations and inventions come about because he is not tied to traditional ways of thinking, and, most of all, because he continually seeks to bring out the inherent flavor of all his ingredients to the highest possible level.

EGGS KUNIO

Kunio's sauce has the alluring fragrance of a mixed bouquet of flowers. Sweetness and umami combine with the barest trace of bitterness (a taste preferred by many adults) for a flavor that is devastatingly rich and deep. The year 2001 saw the inception of a new dish consisting of a "hot-spring egg" coated in this sauce. For his second invitation to the Salone del Gusto (Salon of Taste), an international food exhibition held every two years in Turin, Italy, Kunio presented this dish (*Kunio tamago*, or *Eggs Kunio*) to high acclaim.

"I wanted something that would go well with wine," he explains, "and something that would incorporate both wine and eggs, which I love. Wine was the inspiration for my sauce, and I figured the sauce would go perfectly with a hot *onsen tamago* [hot-spring egg]."

ABOVE: Bamboo tea scoop and holder made by Sen no Rikyu. Stamped with the individuality of its maker, a tea scoop therefore helps define the spirit of a tea ceremony. It was Rikyu who placed the node in middle of the shaft, a once-revolutionary innovation that has become standard practice. Christened "Yahara Doi" after an unknown person, this scoop has an austere dignity. Teiichi used this scoop and displayed the scroll at left at a tea ceremony celebrating his eighty-eighth birthday.

LEFT: A letter from Rikyu to Yabunouchi Kenchu, a fellow student of tea, thanking him for some rice dumplings. The text refers familiarly to the potter Furuta Oribe, Kenchu's brother-in-law and a close friend of both men. The wool cloth with a red design on which the scroll is mounted is said to be from the *jimbaori* (samurai vest worn over armor) of the warlord and ruler Toyotomi Hideyoshi (1536–98).

Many Westerners may be unfamiliar with this method of preparing an egg; the secret lies in the water temperature and cooking time (see page 179). Unlike a soft-boiled egg, the yolk of a hot-spring egg comes out well-set, and the white, silky-smooth and viscid. Such eggs are a breakfast staple at any hot-spring spa in Japan, where they are usually eaten with a light *dashi* stock. In Kunio's version, the harmony of the strong-bodied flavor and the luscious, creamy egg is extra special. The dish must be served piping hot.

Kunio is fond of eggs, and for lunch he'll often ask one of his younger cooks, "Make me a *dashi* egg roll, will you?" This simple but delectable dish consists of scrambled egg mixed with stock and lightly grilled, then rolled up. The secret is to cook a dozen or more thin layers, rolling up each new layer to blend in softly with the rest. Simple as it is, making the dish properly requires finesse, which makes it a good way to test the skills of his junior chefs; this may be another reason why he requests it so often. Either way, when he's eating this dish, Kunio's face is the picture of happiness.

The name *Eggs Kunio* was decided by happenstance. Once, when Kunio was being interviewed for television, the director asked him the name of the dish he was preparing, and he answered off the top of his head, "*Kunio tamago!*" The name stuck, and the dish has become a highly regarded staple in Kunio's culinary repertoire.

HORAKU-YAKI: Bringing in Spring with a Bang

Kitcho's *Horaku-yaki* is prepared in connection with the early February holiday of *setsubun*, which marked the day before spring under the old lunar calendar. The occasion is customarily celebrated by running around chanting, "*Oni wa soto, fuku wa uchi*" ("Out with the demons, in with good luck!") and scattering handfuls of dry-roasted beans. It's also customary for people to eat the same number of beans as their age, plus one more for good luck. Baleful influences (demons) were thought to be prevalent around changes in the season, and throwing beans was a way to drive them off; thus the ceremony is a traditional way to ward off calamity and pray that the entire household will remain healthy and safe through the coming year.

Mibu-dera temple in Kyoto is known for a type of masked, wordless comic play performed in connection with this bean-throwing ritual, and a unique tradition has grown up around it. In early February, people mill around the temple grounds buying unglazed earthenware plates called *horaku*, on which they paint the names and ages of everyone in the family, along with a wish for each person, before offering them to the temple. Later on, as part of *Horaku-wari* ("Plate-smashing"), one of the farces performed for a Buddhist memorial service held from April 21 to 29, the plates offered in February are pushed off the stage and smashed. Having your plate smashed means that you are rid of evil and your wishes will come true.

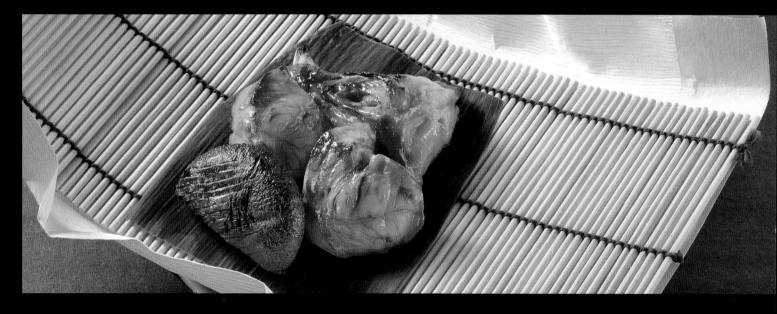

Spicy Blowfish Horaku-yaki. A playful tradition at Kitcho calls for a treat to be hidden under a lid brushed with auspicious calligraphy (left). This time around, hefty nuggets of seasoned and grilled blowfish emerge, to the unfailing delight of the guests.

One day Kunio's father Koji went to see the comic play and came up with an idea for a new way to serve food, which he called *horaku-yaki*. Taking a broad, unglazed earthen platter of the sort used for roasting beans or tea, he placed on it some ready-to-eat food wrapped in thick Japanese paper; on another platter he brushed in red ink the name of the Buddhist memorial service and characters reading "dispel misfortune." Then he laid the second plate over the first as a lid, and popped the whole into a hot oven. When the plates were heated, a guest chosen to wear a traditional comic mask would smash the top with a wooden hammer, revealing the food inside, carefully wrapped to ensure that no shards would come into contact with it. The dry, heated lid would crack open with a satisfyingly loud *bang!*

Koji says, "Teiichi was always telling me to come up with new ideas. When I went to see the Mibu comic play, it hit me: this would make an interesting

food presentation. Other times, I thought up new dishes that were inspired by Japanese confections."

Everyday events or special occasions can be the seeds for new culinary ideas. Keeping one's antennae up at all times, alertly connecting everything to the world of cuisine: this was the stance Teiichi took, which he passed on to his son-in-law and grandson, and which Kunio faithfully upholds to this day.

Horaku-yaki has become another seasonal tradition at Kitcho. Like the cuisine served to celebrate the Doll Festival in spring and the Miscanthus Rings Festival in summer, it is offered in hopes of guests' continued health, safety, and happiness. This time, Kunio has used blowfish glazed with sauce and charcoal-grilled shiitake mushroom (previous page), but the particular food combinations vary. "The only guideline I have is to use foods in season, right at the peak of freshness. If requested, I could even use meat," says Kunio.

When *setsubun* draws near, the head of the restaurant must take time from his busy schedule to brush calligraphy in red on some 150 earthenware lids. For the last dozen years or so, this task has fallen to Kunio.

ABOVE: *Shark Fin Rice Bowl.* The shark fin is simmered in a special chicken stock, then topped with a chicken-flavored, soy-based sauce and garnished with crisped rice, slivered long onion, and a pinch of red pepper. Tender and memorable.

FAR LEFT: *Devil's Tongue Pasta.* These springy noodles made from devil's tongue (*ito konnyaku*) are garnished with a cornucopia of delicious toppings: chopped blowfish, monkfish liver, pistachio halves, and prickly ash leaves (*kinome*). The whole is decorated with gold foil, and the character for "good wishes" is brushed in soy sauce.

Oyster Rice. Aromatic hints of the sea—oysters and kelp stock—mingle with soy sauce in this dish. Oysters are either deep-fried or quickly blanched in hot kelp stock, which is also used for cooking the rice.

THE ROLE OF THE *OKAMI*

At Kitcho, it is Kunio who is in charge of the kitchen. "Cooked food should be delicious as a matter of course, but that's not all," he reflects. "Each guest should feel 'This was made especially for me.' That's what I always tell my staff. But the kitchen is physically separated from the private rooms where the guests are, so the link between the guests and the kitchen is our team of waitresses, headed by the *okami* (proprietess). The *okami* is a central figure in any fine Japanese restaurant."

The *okami* of Kitcho is Kunio's wife Ritsuko, who keeps an eye on the overall operation of the restaurant, from preparation of the rooms to greeting the guests. When there are large parties of guests and the cooking and wait staff are hard pressed, she must remain serene and smiling, issuing an occasional mild instruction and keeping everyone calm and focused. When things are hectic, one word from her is enough to make everyone relax and get back on track.

Says Ritsuko, "I don't think of hospitality as something standard, one-size-fits-all. I try to personalize the hospitality we offer, including the room appointments. I tell this to all the wait staff, and I myself am constantly trying to improve."

For example, a waitress inquires about a diner's preference for saltiness at the soup course, which is usually served second, and conveys that information to the kitchen. That way, the later courses can reflect the diner's individual preference. While exchanging casual talk with guests, the waitress elicits information about their likes and dislikes, as well as the size of serving they prefer. If someone should mention a dislike for fish, for example, the cook will immediately find suitable substitutes. Both the food and the hospitality, in short, must ensure that each guest feels personally welcomed, and knows that a special effort to please has been made. That is the ultimate goal.

The *okami* has the essential—and enormous—task of ensuring that communication between the waitresses and the kitchen is taking place smoothly, and determining whether the guests are truly content. If they are less than perfectly satisfied, it's also her job to figure out why, and to take swift steps to remedy the situation. She must remain constantly on the alert.

As the *okami* sees off the departing guests, her gracious smile and deep bows are by no means mere rote formalities. The atmosphere is charged with a deep sense of thankfulness and joy that she and her guests share. This is the spirit of *ichigo ichi-e*, the awareness that each meeting is a precious, once-in-a-lifetime occasion.

"I'm dealt with in the media a lot, so I stand out," says Kunio, "and people get the idea that Kitcho is all about me. But it's not—it's the *okami* who's the actual face of the restaurant. Without her," he states firmly, "we'd be nothing."

A TYPICAL
KAISEKI LUNCH

Lunch at Kitcho begins at ¥35,000 (over $350), dinner at ¥40,000 (over $400). Each meal consists of set courses that vary in structure, order, number, and contents according to the price level chosen. At the base price, lunch begins with the *hassun* course, a tribute to the season. While the exact details will naturally differ according to the time of year, as well as the guest's preferences and the day's catch, a sample lunch is described below.

Fine cuisine is something to be relished not just with the palate and the eyes, but also with the senses of hearing, smell, and touch. The chef creates a symphony of flavors appealing to the full spectrum of senses, one in which the tone of each individual ingredient is as important as the overall harmony. The careful pairing of food and serving vessel is an important element in achieving this rich harmony. A meal at Kitcho is a total sensual experience.

1. ***Hassun***   Fresh crabmeat with vinegar dressing (*kanisu*), chrysanthemum leaves and thin slices of deep-fried tofu (*abura-age*), baby red shrimp, braised beef tongue, salt-grilled barracuda, shrimp with *moromi* miso, rolled omelet.

2. **Soup**   Sea bream, *matsutake* mushroom, green citron, *udo*.

3. **Sashimi**   Blanched sea-bream sashimi, *iwatake* lichen, chrysanthemum flower, *oka hijiki* ("land seaweed"), radish slices, wasabi.
    Seared tuna, daikon radish, long onion, myoga ginger, perilla flowers and buds, *nori* seaweed, whelk, ginger, *mibuna* (a kind of mustard plant).

4. ***Hashiyasume* ("chopstick rest")**   Steamed *yuba* (soy milk skin) with amber sauce, salt-water eel, *mukago* (small wild yams), onion, and ginger.

5. **Grilled fish**   Salt-grilled tilefish, grilled shiitake mushroom, fried ginkgo nuts, *sudachi* citrus.

6. **Slow-cooked dish**   *Hiryozu* (deep-fried tofu ball), pumpkin, Fushimi-togarashi pepper, winter melon, sword beans, yellow citron.

7. **Rice and pickles**   Rice with *matsutake* mushroom, salt-grilled chicken, turnip and pickled-apricot paste (*bainiku*) mixed with bonito flakes, pickled greens with sesame, salt-pickled eggplant, cucumber, ginger and red *shiso*, seasoned with apricot vinegar and soy sauce.

8. **Fruit**   Melon, Pione grapes, fig, La France pear, raspberries.

9. **Green tea and confections**   *Hatsukari* (kudzu dumpling flavored with brown sugar).

1. *Hassun*

A Kitcho-style *hassun* uses colorful flowers, leaves, and the like to celebrate the season with flair. The strong visual impact of this course heightens expectations for what will follow. Flavoring is simple so that the diner can enjoy the full, unmasked flavor of each ingredient. A vinegared dish is always included to stir the appetite and refresh the palate.

2. **Soup**

The soup course is of central importance in the meal, its appeal based on the freshness and quality of ingredients as well as the flavor of the soup stock. The very simplicity of the presentation demands perfection.

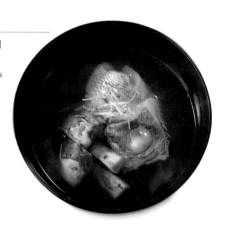

3. **Sashimi**

Slices of succulent raw fish are one of the highlights of the kaiseki meal. Here above all, supreme quality and freshness are essential. The first plate contains light-flavored fish such as sea bream, globefish, or flounder.

The second plate features tuna, squid, spiny lobster (*Ise ebi*), and other richly flavored seafood that goes well with strong condiments.

4. *Hashiyasume* ("chopstick rest")

The purpose of this course is to introduce a side dish that contrasts in flavor, texture, and so on with the dishes that have come before. As this marks the dividing point between the first and second halves of the menu, unusual flavors are eschewed in favor of milder "comfort" foods.

5. **Grilled fish**

The second half of the meal starts off with grilled fish. Fine fresh fish that would also make excellent sashimi is served not raw but rare, with extreme care taken not to overcook it. Ordinarily the fish is salt-grilled to bring out its essential flavor, but sometimes in winter a marinade is used.

6. **Slow-cooked dish**

Toward the end of the meal, vegetables come into their own. Diners savor the goodness of cooked vegetables in this medley. In summertime, the vegetables are often grilled rather than simmered.

7. **Rice and pickles**

This course rounds out the meal. Rice should be served within ten minutes after cooking. To ensure that this happens, the kitchen staff counts back to calculate exactly where in the meal to begin cooking the rice.

Pickles, or *konomono*, are an indispensable accompaniment to rice. Usually three kinds are selected, of contrasting colors and textures.

8. **Fruit**

For dessert, a supreme luxury: carefully selected fruits harvested at the very peak of ripeness. Kitcho staff often set out early in the morning for local farms and orchards that provide the restaurant with fruit under special license.

9. **Green tea and confections**

After the meal proper, in order to invite guests to linger and enjoy the pleasant reverberations of a fine dining experience over after-dinner conversation, green tea and Japanese-style confections are served.

On approaching the restaurant, the guest is
greeted at the entrance to the grounds by a
modest sign announcing Kitcho's presence,
a calligraphic effort of Teiichi's in his ninety-
first year. From the first moment to the last,
"tasteful" remains the byword.

THE KAISEKI KITCHEN

Inside Kitcho

Behind-the-scenes bustle at Kitcho.

Arashiyama is a busy place, always thronged with sightseers. However, in a quiet corner just a few steps away from the foot of celebrated Togetsukyo Bridge stands a large wooden gate marking the entrance to Kitcho. Stepping inside, you enter a different world—a world of superlative grace and beauty where fine cuisine, tableware, décor, and service banish workaday cares.

Behind the scenes at Kitcho is yet another realm, one where voices call back and forth to check on the progress of the meal, and kimono-clad waitresses scurry to and fro. This highly charged atmosphere, so different from the elegant veneer of tranquil gardens and private dining rooms, reveals another face of Kitcho.

In this section we will go behind the scenes for an in-depth look at how the quality at Kitcho is maintained through the cultivation of change—a constant refining of flavor and structure.

Courage to Uphold Old Traditions, Courage to Instill New Ones

"What I really wanted to do," says Kunio, "was to *be* my grandfather." When he resolved to carry on the restaurant founded by his grandfather, he aimed for the peak of the profession. To reach such a level Kunio, too, needed to be recognized as a charismatic presence and a revolutionary force in the world of Japanese cuisine.

But not long after he returned to Arashiyama in the late 1980s, having completed his training at Kitcho restaurants in Osaka and Tokyo, he found the restaurant's continued existence in doubt after the excesses and ultimate collapse of Japan's bubble economy. When the bubble burst in the early 1990s, fine old eating establishments around the country were hard hit, and even Kitcho, at the summit of the Japanese culinary world, began to wobble precariously. None of the plans undertaken to remedy the situation had any effect. Things went from bad to worse, with no relief in sight.

In those hard times, the pressure on Kunio as the new executive chef was intense. Some people seemed to hold him personally responsible for the restaurant's management crisis. What provided a way out from that rock bottom low, he now recalls, was the liberating realization of a simple fact: he was not, and never would be, his grandfather Teiichi. Charged with carrying on the legacy of Teiichi's Kitcho brand, Kunio had become obsessed with the need to faithfully imitate all that his grandfather had done. But that was in fact impossible; he could no more act exactly like Teiichi than he could look like him. The way to preserve Kitcho tradition was not to slavishly follow the forms that Teiichi had laid out, but rather to stay true to the intentions behind them. That realization led Kunio to implement reforms that revitalized the restaurant.

Teiichi at 80 with a 21-year-old Kunio in 1982.

It struck him that Teiichi had been among the first to incorporate nontraditional foods such as caviar and foie gras into his recipes, and had gone on inventing original, innovative dishes for as long as he lived. Such willingness to implement change was the very Kitcho tradition he, Kunio, should be seeking to uphold.

Some things, of course, could not be changed—the sense of the seasons reflected in the foods prepared, for example, along with the celebration of seasonal events. The buildings in classical *sukiya-zukuri* architectural style remain in use today; and the antique furnishings, utensils, and tableware hand-crafted by master artisans of the past are all lovingly preserved. But knowing what to change and what to keep isn't always easy. Even now that the restaurant is on a solid managerial footing, hidden struggles take place daily as Kunio continues to formulate his own style while coping with the tension between tradition and innovation.

Some things at Kitcho remain constant, unchanging.

Traditional Flavor Isn't Static

One of the lessons Kunio learned through painful experience was the danger of blindly following tradition. To keep a tradition from stagnating, it's important to go back and examine the meaning behind it. To do that, one must appreciate the value of doubt.

For example, Kunio came to embrace doubts about the two-hundred-year-old tradition of flavoring rice with vinegar for hand-shaped sushi (*nigiri-zushi*). Because each sushi chef is particular about what condiments he mixes with the vinegar, and in what proportions, the flavor of the sushi rice varies subtly from place to place. Yet within every establishment, a single flavoring is used for all types of sushi, whether made with slabs of red-fleshed fish, white-fleshed fish, shellfish, or any other topping. Kunio wondered if one flavor was really enough. Wouldn't it be better to vary the acidity for rich, fatty fare

like *toro* (tuna belly) and lighter fare like flounder? And why use only distilled vinegars such as rice vinegar? Out of this line of thinking came a refreshing new style of hand-shaped sushi using *sudachi* (a small, green Japanese citrus), lemon, lime, and other citrus juices to season the rice under white-fleshed fish.

Is the old way of doing things invariably the best way? Couldn't there be a better approach? Such questions lie also at the heart of the tea ceremony, Kunio believes, which through the centuries has adapted and changed in pursuit of ever-finer etiquette for ever-more perfect hospitality.

The very idea of "unchanging flavor" is an illusion, he avers. Unlike factory-produced items, nature's bounty can never be truly homogeneous. Individual fish of the same variety and place of production each have a distinctive flavor, as do apples from the same tree. Conditions change day by day, making food "the same as yesterday" an unattainable goal. All the more unreasonable, then, to expect that Kunio could re-create the exact cuisine of Teiichi's day.

The same is true of *dashi* stock, that unshakable cornerstone of Japanese cuisine. In an attempt to maintain continuity with the past, Kunio might religiously use kelp and bonito from the same region and the same producers as Teiichi had, but since natural products cannot maintain uniform quality over time, the taste would inevitably be different. Just as Teiichi selected the finest ingredients of his time, so Kunio needs to seek out the finest ingredients available today, taking advantage of new information, knowledge, and systems to come up with the tastiest possible *dashi* stock. That is Kunio's method and his interpretation of Kitcho style, a way of thinking that brought him to devise his improved recipe for *dashi* stock.

The time-honored method, which was followed at Kitcho for many years, is to place sheets of kelp in cold water and heat them over a medium flame, pulling the kelp out and add-

Soaking kelp in the first stage of *dashi* production.

After the kelp is removed, bonito flakes are added to the simmering broth.

ing bonito flakes just before the water reaches a boil. After a research institution announced that the optimum way of drawing out kelp's glutamate—the source of its umami—was to simmer it for an hour at 150° F (65 °C), many chefs quickly followed suit. To Kunio, however, the result tasted poor. Even if the glutamate was fully extracted, other active ingredients must interfere with the flavor, he reasoned. Based on this analysis, he ran his own experiments until by trial and error he came up with a new way: he leaves the kelp to soak overnight in cold water, then takes the stock from the refrigerator, removes the kelp, and heats the liquid. Experimentation taught him that a water temperature of 40 °F (5 °C) was best, and that soaking for sixteen hours yielded the purest distillation of flavor. The advice of kelp growers also influenced his conclusions.

As this example shows, relying blindly on the latest information and scientific theories can be dangerous. In the end, the only meaningful test of flavor lies in human taste buds: a chef must make judgments based on his own sampling of food. Improvements in flavor require extensive experimentation.

The Evolution of Culinary Arts Based on Science

Kunio, who fully appreciates the scientific aspects of cooking, is a fiend for experimentation. Whenever he obtains a piece of interesting new information, or a new ingredient of some kind, the Kitcho kitchens are transformed on the spot into testing laboratories.

One day, Kunio had his young cooking staff make shrimp cutlets using two different kinds of batter. For *tonkatsu* (deep-fried pork cutlet), the meat is coated in flour, then dipped in beaten whole egg before being covered in bread crumbs. The question at hand was whether the same approach was best for a shrimp cutlet as well. Kunio decided to compare shrimp cutlets made with whole-egg batter and egg-white batter. After sampling each, he gave the nod to the cutlet made using only egg white. The richer taste of the yolk, he decided, interfered with the flavor of the shrimp, which is lighter than that of pork.

Advances in nutritional science have made possible the verification of many traditional food benefits—including the mechanism that makes the kelp-bonito combination in *dashi* stock so satisfying. Combined, the glutamic acid in kelp and the inosinic acid in bonito flakes are known to increase the brain's output of pleasure neurochemicals like beta-endorphins as much as sevenfold, thus greatly enhancing the perception of umami. This helps explain why Japanese food is delicious and satisfying even though fats and dairy products are not used. In fact, a kaiseki meal is just as filling as a Western full-course meal, with less than half the calories (approximately 700, as opposed to about 1500). This is one of the many health benefits of Japanese cookery.

Glutamate-inosinate combinations are found all over the world. Glutamate is present in tomatoes, hard cheese, and mushrooms, inosinate in red meat and fish. Dishes combining tomatoes and fish or cheese and meat are popular in the West. The prevalence of this same glutamate-inosinate combination in the West, and the scientific research explaining it, gave Kunio the idea of mixing Western and Japanese ingredients in dishes like *Sirloin Sashimi Seasoned with Kelp* (page 145).

The knowledge that different proteins harden at different temperatures inspired Kunio to make another new recipe. For beef, pork, and other meat, protein solidifies at around 150 °F (65 °C). Knowing this led Kunio to speculate that for the classic hot pot dish *shabu-shabu*, it might be better not to let the stock come to a boil, but to swish the thin meat slices in broth at that low temperature. Through experimentation he found that meat prepared this way was both attractive in color and tasty, with an appealing texture and a maximum of savory umami. At higher temperatures, meat toughens, and longer cooking times destroy umami. The dish he created based on this understanding is *Low-Temperature Sukiyaki* (page 148).

In the case of eggs, the white and yolk harden at different temperatures: the yolk at 150–158 °F (65–70 °C), and the white at 167–172 °F (75–78 °C). An *onsen-tamago* (hot-spring egg; see Food Notes for page 79) is made by taking advantage of this difference. By the same token, in other dishes where a whole egg would ordinarily be added, Kunio puts in the white and the yolk separately, giving the white a little extra time to cook. Doing so brings out the bright gold of the yolk and preserves the best flavor of both parts of the egg. *Goby and Egg Scramble* (page 24) is an example.

Aroma and texture are traditionally considered key attributes of fine food. Kunio's awareness of these factors was heightened by the knowledge that they can be verified scientifically. Flavor aside, aroma and texture also affect the perception of deliciousness. Taste receptors in the mouth that respond to umami and sweetness are of a single kind each, but there are many more—around fifty—for bitterness. However, in the nose there are some 380 kinds of smell receptors, and there are innumerable receptors for texture in the mouth. Two foods with the same flavor constituents will thus be perceived as completely unrelated if their aroma and texture are different. This explains why sashimi made from even the finest fish loses its appeal if it is sliced with a dull knife: the flavor elements are overwhelmed by texture.

Understanding how the brain processes flavor led Kunio to revisit older recipes, adding aroma and texture with varied garnishes, as in *Pan-Roasted Rice Balls* (page 15) and *Sirloin Sashimi Seasoned with Kelp* (page 145); or by grilling food on only one side, as in *Grilled Summer Vegetables* (page 65) and *Shark Fin Turtle Soup* (page 92). New knowledge inspires him to conduct new experiments. The results of his constant endeavors are reflected in the recipes at Kitcho, which continue to evolve.

Out with "Common Sense"

Another lesson Kunio has learned is that dispensing with fixed ideas and so-called common sense opens up new possibilities. For one thing, this revelation led him to begin pairing wine with Japanese cuisine. In times past, restaurants that set great store by tradition would never mix Japanese and Western food or drink. Today, however, it's not at all unusual to do so. Kitcho began to serve wine in the late 1980s, partly in response to guests' requests. The restaurant went so far as to add on a wine cellar where the temperature is kept constant year round—a pioneering innovation for a traditional Japanese establishment. Today the wine cellar holds nearly 2,000 bottles, including champagnes such as Krug Clos du Mesnil 1992 and Jacques Selosse Substance; white wines like Ladoucette Baron de L 2002; and red wines such as Romane Conti 1985, Château Le Pin 1999, and Château Lafite 1945. There are even California wines such as Stag's Leap and Harlan Estate. Kunio's personal selection formed the basis for this abundant array of delicious wines.

The wine cellar at Kitcho.

Some guests enjoy wine with their meal from beginning to end; in such cases, Kunio actually plans menus to accompany the wine, rather than the other way around. Ingredients like olive oil, butter, and cheese are traditionally eschewed in Japanese cooking, but Kunio feels that if they can enhance a

dish they should be used. His *Steamed Custard with Two Cheeses* (page 28), using two varieties of cheese, has the authentic flavor of Japanese *chawanmushi*, a popular savory custard, thanks to the strength of the *dashi* stock in it. Kunio has even come up with an original recipe for kelp stock using butter, which he named "So-fumi" (the name is derived from *so*, a cheese-like ingredient from the Heian period (794–1185), and *fumi*, which means "flavor"). He uses this stock often in dishes that go well with wine, such as *Mélange of Spring Greens* (page 36) and *Shrimp Potato Croquette* (page 97).

Renewing Ingredients

A cook with the flexibility to use new information without being bound to entrenched ideas—things "everybody knows"—can create new recipes without limit. But the key to good flavor ultimately lies in the quality of the ingredients. That's why Kunio roams the country in search of the best in foods and condiments. Back in his grandfather's day, when the transportation network and distribution system were not as well developed as they are today, having such a range of choices was unthinkable.

When Kunio does come across an ingredient that he deems the best in its category, he won't adopt it permanently, but remains alert to ever-better possibilities, constantly picking and choosing. Nature's offerings, even those from an identical source, vary in quality from season to season depending on the conditions in which they grew. Moreover, settling on one item exclusively eliminates the possibility of encountering something even better.

The blind rice-tasting test that began at Kitcho a few years ago in this spirit has become a celebrated event. Every fall, samples of the year's finest rice pour in from around the country and everyone sits down to compare them: Kunio and his wife, the kitchen staff, waitresses, sometimes even the growers. The one that gains the highest overall rating will be laid in for the coming year. Samples start coming in October and November, when the first crops of new rice are harvested, beginning with the southernmost regions and moving steadily north. The samples are carefully reviewed and twenty or so chosen, after which the kitchen staff winnows them down further to a handful. These finalists are cooked to the same degree of hardness, and everyone tries each one to see which is the best. The samples are judged on taste, aroma, tone, glossiness, texture, and so on; just-cooked rice, cooked rice that has been kept hot an extra ten minutes, and cold rice are all checked. With so many factors to rate, there is no guarantee that the sample scoring highest in the "just-cooked" category will necessarily win. The results of the test are announced in December, and the winning rice is used starting at New Year's. For the last three years, incidentally, the top-rated rice has been Koshihikari, from Niigata Prefecture.

With such care taken in the selection of rice at Kitcho, cooks are naturally very fussy about how the rice is prepared and served. For every private dining room, a copper cooking pot is readied, its size chosen according to the number of guests. The cooking process is timed to the progress of each individual meal, so that the rice will always be ready just in time. Each pot is constantly watched by one person until the rice is ready to eat. At Kitcho, rice is served immediately, without being allowed to sit and steam. Kunio calls this "al dente," maintaining that rice offering a slight resistance when you bite into it is richer in aroma and texture.

Sources for kelp and bonito, too, may change now and then as various staff members occasionally pay visits to learn more about the localities where they are produced. Just recently, Kunio brought back several varieties of kelp from his travels and organized another blind taste test. Everyone on hand gathered to try various styles of stock made using the different kinds of kelp. On such occasions, if any of the newer kinds is found to be superior to the kelp already in use, a change is made. Partly because two different kinds of kelp are used in the course of the year anyway (one for summer and one for winter), changes occur over a fairly short span of time.

Salt, soy sauce, and other such condiments are switched much less frequently—certainly not once a year. Still, for natural sea salt, as many as six different varieties are carefully selected, each for a different purpose: grilled food, simmered food, broth, pickles, and so on. Soy sauce is generally made to order from whole organic soybeans, and now and then the entire stock is replaced. Specially made soy sauce is used, not only because of the Kitcho insistence on fine flavor, but because

Rice is constantly supervised while it cooks.

of the assurance that comes from knowing the ingredients and their producer thoroughly.

Sake served at Kitcho includes their original brand, Kitcho Teio, a premium grade classified as *mutenka daiginjo* (additive-free pure rice wine made from grains that have been polished at least 50%; in general, the higher the degree of polishing, the higher the quality), as well as Shinsei and Matsu no Midori, top products of the venerable Yamamoto Honke sake brewery in Fushimi, Kyoto. These are all used for cooking as well as drinking. The lees from making Kitcho Teio are also used in cooking (see page 144).

Even specially ordered foods are subject to constant improvement. At Kitcho, the search is always underway for something greater, and whenever a food or drink of superlative quality and trustworthiness is found, it is added to the larder or replaces something else. The process of change and renewal never ends.

Food Suppliers and *Shun*

Teiichi called his own cooking "a model of the seasons." To provide cuisine that conveys a strong sense of the season, the chef must have access to fresh ingredients right at the peak of ripeness and flavor—what the Japanese call *shun*. In the early 1990s, just as Kunio was beginning to feel apprehensive about the continued availability of high-quality seasonal foods, he asked around at farmers' cooperatives and public offices for places that grew produce without agricultural chemicals. He found only one in all Kyoto: Nagasawa Farm in Uzumasa. Gen'ichi Nagasawa, the seventeenth-generation owner of the four-hundred-year-old farm, had repeatedly fallen ill while spraying agricultural chemicals, and so had no choice but to begin making organic, chemical-free produce on his own. In the beginning his neighbors thought he was crazy. He says it took three years to restore the natural balance of the soil in his fields. Toughing out a difficult period without income, after eight years he was able to produce stable cash crops. It was in this eighth year that he began dealing with Kitcho.

The vegetables from Nagasawa Farm are brimming with vitality, as if all the earth's energy flowed into them. Now that chemical-free vegetables are all the rage, and thanks in part to Kunio's vouching, Nagasawa's produce is in high demand. His finest okra sells for twice the going price; Kunio uses it in Kitcho's *Cold Turtle Soup* (page 58) and *Water Shield Leaf in Tosa Vinegar* (page 61).

According to public perception, chemical-free produce features fruits and vegetables with worm-eaten leaves and a

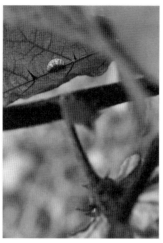

Checking the vegetables at Kitagawa's farm.

Ladybug larvae keep pests away from eggplant.

generally poor appearance. Nagasawa, however, is of the firm opinion that "truly delicious food is also beautiful to look at," and brooks no compromise in his quest for beauty as well as flavor. He gives Kitcho less than ten percent of his harvest— only the portion that he himself judges to be the best. Despite a strong stubborn streak, he shares his technical knowledge and skills freely and has acquired a number of followers.

One such follower is Norishige Kitagawa, a former company worker who gave up his job to take up organic chemical-free gardening in nearby Keihoku-cho, Kyoto. Kitagawa puts his heart into his work, starting by working rice bran, chaff, and fallen leaves into the soil to make hot compost. He says that exercising his ingenuity to experiment with different ratios of nitrogen and carbon, or different temperatures, gives him endless pleasure. When the soil maintains the proper balance of microbes and the field's immunity rises, there are enough beneficial insects to cancel out the harmful ones, obviating any need for chemicals. Ladybug larvae, for example, are beneficial for eggplant leaves, and he makes the rounds regularly, checking eagerly for their presence. The snap peas in *Mélange of Spring Greens* (page 36) are from Kitagawa's farm. When you pick one of his peas and bite into it, there is a satisfying crispness followed by a burst of sweetness and umami. "But at this time of year," he laments, "all they'll take is my snap peas." In order to increase the selection of vegetables that meet Kitcho's strict standards, he is constantly conducting experiments to improve the levels of flavor and beauty in his produce.

In this way, the celebrated "Kitcho flavor" originates in the oceans and fields where unsung heroes labor in the frontlines of primary industry. Kitcho's kitchen is connected not just with growers in the immediate vicinity, but with centers of production around the country.

The Kitcho Brand and Japanese Society

In the early 1990s, while he was touring the country visiting premier production sites in search of ingredients, Kunio began to feel a tremor of panic. In agriculture, fishing, and animal husbandry alike, Japan was facing a crisis of sufficient magnitude to permanently alter the nation's diet. Top priority was being given to economic factors alone, and the sort of careful, labor-intensive work that produces food of high quality was being shunted aside. For example, *katsuobushi* (blocks of smoke-cured bonito) made the old-fashioned way took six months to dry properly, and faced stiff competition from a cheaper, inferior product made more quickly using dryers. Without any guarantee of income, elderly workmen were unable to attract apprentices and so had no way to pass their skills on to the next generation. Their precious know-how was on the verge of disappearing.

Economizing is important, but what is the real cost of undermining a nation's diet and the natural environment that supports it? Realizing with deep concern that the problem was far bigger than Kitcho, Kunio sprang into action. He began to speak out on the state of food producers—people who are normally removed from the public eye—serving as a conduit between them and the public. Moreover, he stressed repeatedly that the key to saving Japanese food culture was to make primary industry an attractive career choice. He had heroic figures like Nagasawa tell their life stories, and he participated in projects related to food production. At the same time, he came to see that the Kitcho brand name, and the trust it represented, could be used to serve society in practical ways.

Kunio aimed his efforts to raise awareness not only in Japanese society at large but also in centers of food production. In the northern Kyoto city of Kyotango, which he knew well from his dealings there to purchase snow crab, he joined a policy planning committee, so that he could help local fishermen able to catch crab only in the wintertime generate ways to stabilize their livelihood. From his ideas for products with added value to suggestions for improved fishing methods, Kunio has been making an impact on local awareness.

As a natural extension of such activities, he became involved in culinary events overseas. With the hope in mind that worldwide recognition for Japanese cuisine will help to revitalize the country's primary industry, he participates in such events as often as he can. Through venues like the "Umami Summit" held in San Francisco and London, and the "Salone del Gusto" in Italy, he has forged invaluable ties with top chefs from around the world, and they have found that visiting one another's establishments and exchanging opinions offers great mutual stimulation. Thomas Keller of the French Laundry in Napa Valley, Heston Blumenthal of the Fat Duck in Berkshire, Ferran Adrià of elBulli in Catalonia, Spain—each has a deep appreciation of Japanese haute cuisine. Kunio hopes to be able to work together with people like these, not only to enhance their respective cuisines, but to increase world awareness of the need to preserve food culture and the environment.

Kitcho Staff Who Support the Kitcho Brand

Presently Kitcho is run by a staff of thirty-one, working under Kunio and his wife Ritsuko: nineteen cooks, nine waitresses, and three office workers. During the slump following the collapse of the bubble economy, Kunio took a hard look not at the food or ingredients at Kitcho, but at the employment and training of its staff. In the belief that people are the most important element in the organization, they began by training young people. After their reforms were implemented, the average age of their cooks dropped to 24.

In Japan, the traditional relationship between master chef and sub-chef has been that of master and disciple, a severely hierarchical arrangement with many innate flaws. Kunio sought to change this. For example, under the old system the disciple was supposed to learn techniques passively by observing his master and seniors at work, but the inefficiency of this system led Kunio to introduce a policy of thorough and painstaking instruction. In addition, unlike the old days, young cooks are also given important work to do. Of course, the positive features of the traditional style of training were retained.

For the first year, members of the kitchen staff are kept busy with jobs such as polishing pans, scrubbing floors, and cleaning. In between times they are given opportunities to cook, and can home their skills if they are so inclined. Those who prove to be apt learners, paying attention to their surroundings and thinking on their feet, move on to become *gesokuban*, or door-

men, a job too important to entrust to complete beginners. A doorman must sprinkle water in the garden and over the concrete portion of the entryway just before guests arrive or leave, put away their footwear when they enter, and set it out again unerringly when they go. He serves as gardener, porter, and car valet, doing all in his power to make guests' arrivals and departures as smooth as possible. This portion of training lasts six months, out of a conviction that cooks, too, need experience in dealing personally with guests. Next the apprentice is assigned to one of four kitchen posts (grilling, *hassun*, boiling, or sashimi) to learn cooking techniques in earnest while delving into the particulars of each specialty.

Beginning in the early 1990s, Kitcho required women waiting on tables (*nakai*) to have a college education. At about the same time, the restaurant began running want ads for *nakai* over the Internet. These were earthshaking changes in a field where such workers were traditionally hired based solely on personal connections. As overseas guests increased, it became necessary to have wait staff fluent in foreign languages. At the same time, the job requires an understanding of Japanese history and culture, the ability to enhance one's education, and a constant drive for self-improvement.

As part of their entrance ceremony, newly hired employees listen to a lecture by the late Zen master Soko Morinaga of Myoshinji, a Rinzai-sect Zen temple. Formerly they heard him speak in person, but since Morinaga's death in 1995 the lecture has been presented on video. Kunio insists on keeping up this tradition so that the entire staff is united in their desire to make Kitcho the best it can be, and so that each individual may take the initiative, however he or she can, to make that happen. The master taught the entire family, beginning with Teiichi. After Kunio left home at age twenty, wanting to become a musician, Morinaga took him in at his Zen temple and, through rigorous training, helped him gain the resolve to take over the family business. He was truly a "life teacher."

A doorman splashes water at the entry way.

Kitcho employees are encouraged to study traditional arts like calligraphy.

Influenced by Kunio's strong example, Kitcho staff seek to acquire expertise in advanced culinary arts and service and to become culturally grounded, striving not only on the job but in their free time to achieve greater technical prowess and to train themselves in mind and spirit. The restaurant willingly helps with the cost of lessons in tea ceremony, flower arrangement, and other traditional arts or disciplines, as well as sponsoring lessons in calligraphy. Employees take full advantage of such opportunities.

Waitresses must be prepared to answer guests' questions, so before each meal they study information about the ingredients and where they were produced as well as the relevant cooking techniques, tableware, room appointments, and so on. Behind the scenes, one can often come upon a young woman engrossed in studying right up to the moment the meal begins. Without a broad base of knowledge as a foundation, of course, her job would be impossible.

One of the most important tasks for waitresses is *haizukuri*, the cleaning of the ash used in the incense burners and elsewhere in the dining rooms and during tea making. In August, all the ash from the past year is gathered, washed in water, and laid out to dry on straw mats in the blazing sun. *Bancha* tea is poured over the ash again and again to improve its color and aroma. Between dousings, it is allowed to dry. The women protect themselves from the summer heat with sun-hats and towels wrapped around their necks. Taking care of even this smallest detail is a form of spiritual training. In the world of the tea ceremony, *haizukuri* is considered extremely important.

Diligence in the kitchen starts with maintaining cooking utensils in prime condition so that they are both easy to use and pleasing to the eye. The sharpness of kitchen knives, in particular, is so essential that knife-sharpening is said to be the start of all cooking. Maintaining knives prop-

Ash is washed and laid out to dry on straw mats.

erly is so basic that someone is always at it, sharpening knives the last thing at night and the first thing in the morning.

Often the staff is called on to use their wits to improvise when the exact tool needed is unavailable. For example, the number and size of the holes in the lid of a salt shaker must be adjusted depending on the type of fish or meat being cooked. Furthermore, special grills for *dengaku*—tofu that is grilled

Checking the condition of a knife before using.

over coals and coated with miso—are handmade in various sizes to match the size of the tofu. Those for sweetfish (page 70) are adjusted by hand to match the length of the fish; Kitcho is especially particular about this. Cooks therefore need to know a few handyman's tricks.

Japanese meals always end with a fixed expression of appreciation, "*Gochisosama*," which means literally, "It was a banquet." The original meaning of the root word *chiso* is "run around," and so, since those preparing a banquet run around scouting for the best ingredients for their guests, the word took on the added meaning of hosting a meal. It's particularly fitting at Kitcho, where the staff does indeed run all around the countryside for that very purpose. Mulberry leaves in summer, pampas grass in fall, coral evergreen at New Year's—as far as possible, such seasonal decorations for *hassun* trays and *tokonoma* alcoves are gathered early in the morning from nearby land whose owners have signed agreements with Kitcho. Workers quickly become knowledgeable about what grows wild on which part of a mountain, when it will be ready to harvest, and what shape it's in.

"Sparing no time or effort for fine flavor" might be the motto of Kitcho kitchen workers, who make luxury delicacies like *karasumi* (salt-cured mullet roe) and *suzuko* (salmon roe cured with soy sauce and *dashi*) by hand. *Karasumi* means "Chinese inkstick"; apparently the shape of this gourmet food resembles inksticks imported from Tang-dynasty (618–907) China. The season begins in mid-fall, when around a hundred top-quality mullet egg sacs are brought in every year. When the first batch of fresh

The size and number of holes in the lids of salt shakers depends on the food being cooked.

roe arrives from the seaside prefecture of Wakayama, preparations begin immediately. Needles are inserted into each pouch to painstakingly remove every tiny vein and red speckle that would otherwise show through the transparent skin. It is a mind-boggling chore, but unless this is done, the finished product won't have the proper clear orange color. After being deveined, the roe is smothered in salt and pickled, then dried until it reaches the proper hardness.

The sum total of the patience and devotion that each person gives to his or her work while making light of the difficulty it entails is what makes the distinctive "Kitcho flavor" possible. The kitchen at Kitcho is a place to learn culinary techniques and polish one's sensibilities, but beyond that, it is an arena for spiritual growth and the nurturing of patience.

Preparing *karasumi* for curing.

Hospitality in Action

Kitcho hospitality begins the moment a guest makes a reservation. Various courses differentiated by price are available, but in each case the menu is deliberately left unspecified. Keeping quiet about the details ahead of time increases anticipation and excitement. To ensure that the meal is suited to guests' needs and wishes, information is collected at the time of the reservation concerning favorite foods, allergies or dislikes, salt intake requirements, and so on. What is the occasion for the gathering? Is it a birthday party, perhaps, or a business meeting? Who will be coming and why? Based on detailed questions like these, an information card is drawn up for each guest. On subsequent visits, previous cards are reviewed with care to ensure that details of the food and decor do not overlap unnecessarily.

Once guests' wishes are clear, Kunio uses them to draw up a menu. A whiteboard in the kitchen lists the menu for each private dining room, often annotated: "One likes to drink, one doesn't," for example. The pace of the meal differs depending on whether someone is drinking or not, so this is a vital bit of information. To ensure that food is served with the best possible timing, the waitresses and cooks need to take such factors into account and stay in constant communication. Another time the memo may read, "One no seafood, one no beef, one all OK." It often happens that people sharing a meal at the same table are served entirely different foods from start to finish.

In the seven private dining rooms, preparations are also underway for the guests' arrival. First the rooms are thoroughly cleaned, and the decorative alcove (*tokonoma*) of each one is decorated with an appropriate hanging scroll, flower arrangement, and ornament. If a celebration of some kind is underway, this will be reflected in the scroll; every effort is made to tailor the setting to the occasion. Ritsuko, as the proprietress, does the final inspection. Thirty minutes before the guests' arrival, the waitress in charge adjusts the temperature in their room; it's also her job to calculate the right time to light incense so that a faint scent will gently permeate the room when the guests walk in.

As the hour approaches, doormen gather by the gate to greet the arrivals, take their luggage if necessary, and hold up old-fashioned oiled-paper umbrellas in case of rain. Guests are shown to the entrance, where their personal waitress is kneeling formally, waiting for them. When the meal begins, she keeps an eye on its progress, deciding when to clear the table and when to bring in the next dish. At this stage it sometimes happens that someone reveals, "I can't eat crab," or "Today's our fiftieth wedding anniversary." The waitress swiftly passes this information on to the kitchen, where appropriate adjustments to the menu are made. Slips in timing can ruin a meal, so the waitress must remain focused at all times, her attention never wavering. As waitress' voices resonate in the kitchen, reporting on the progress of each meal, the cooking staff go nimbly about their business in response. The teamwork is finely coordinated.

In the meantime, Ritsuko proceeds from room to room, greeting the guests as they dine and checking on how things are going. It is also her job to see guests off and evaluate their level of satisfaction. When they depart, she goes along with

The tailored menu for each group is listed and carefully tracked on a board in the kitchen.

their waitress to escort them to the front gate and bow with sincere expressions of farewell.

Afterward, the waitress fills out the guest cards with notes about the day's meal, the room decoration, and any new information—including individual levels of satisfaction—before returning them to the office. These cards are a treasured resource at Kitcho.

Eighty Years at Kitcho

In November 2010, the Kitcho group celebrated its eightieth anniversary. Kunio, as head of six Kitcho establishments (including, besides the original Arashiyama restaurant, branches in Gion, Kyoto; Hotel Granvia, Kyoto Station; Yawata City, Kyoto; Midland Square, Nagoya Station; and Windsor Hotel, Hokkaido), is even more determined to demonstrate to the world the beauty of Japanese fine dining and meticulous service, under the shared slogan "Japanese Cuisine, the Pride of the World." That catchphrase came to Teiichi in 1961, during a dark period after the loss of his wife, Kiku. At the time it seemed a fantasy far removed from reality. For example, at the first Tokyo Summit in 1979, when Teiichi catered a state dinner for the first time, squeamish organizers prohibited him from using "raw fish." Yet today the word "sushi" is recognized around the globe, and raw fish is commonly consumed overseas.

In the fall of 2009, at a time when Japanese cuisine was increasingly being judged by Western standards, the first-ever Michelin Guide for the Kyoto-Osaka area came out, further impressing Kunio with how far Japanese cuisine had risen in the world's estimation. Of the seven restaurants awarded the top three-star rating in the guide, six—including Arashiyama Kitcho—specialized in Japanese cuisine.

Such an honor being given to the Arashiyama restaurant represents the fulfillment of Teiichi's dream that someday the world would come to appreciate Japanese kaiseki cuisine. The rating left Kunio marveling at Teiichi's prescience more than fifty years ago, and filled him with a renewed sense of responsibility. New and greater efforts to transmit information remain necessary for the world to gain a better understanding of the true quality and depth of Japanese cuisine as a holistic culture. And naturally, Kitcho must be maintained at the highest level possible.

Whether Kunio's two sons will take over the restaurant remains to be seen. Preparations are underway for a new beginning in the restaurant's eighty-first year, so that eventually, when the next generation comes of age, the name "Kitcho" will be everywhere synonymous with "Japanese Cuisine, the Pride of the World."

On Rice and Japanese *Dashi* Stock

On Rice: Flavor, Fragrance, and Texture Tell the Story
Like musical and dramatic performances, multi-course meals—whether French or Italian or kaiseki—are constructed in stages that build with a quickening tempo toward a climax, followed by a satisfying resolution. During the parade of courses in a Western meal, bread appears after the appetizer and is whisked away once the main course ends. What distinguishes kaiseki cuisine is that the carbohydrate—rice—heralds the end of the meal. Despite changing eating habits, rice remains a major staple in Japan, and Japanese diners are strict in their appraisal. In a meal, it is a standard-bearer—a benchmark. The note sounded by the rice must therefore be clear and refreshing.

At Kitcho, rice is never neglected. The better the rice at the end of the meal, the better it reflects on all that came before, so great pains are taken with its preparation. Kunio sums it up this way: "It makes me happy when customers say every dish is delicious, but when they eat their rice at the end and say 'Ah, that was great! Now I'm really satisfied!' then I know their pleasure is real." For him, cooked rice, if properly prepared, is also fine cuisine.

Kunio and his chefs go to great lengths to bring customers that ultimate sense of satisfaction with a defining endnote of tender, delicate short-grain rice. As soon as the harvest is over, they select the rice to be used in the coming year via blind tasting, considering not only flavor but also fragrance and texture. The best rice offers a fresh and pleasing taste: sweet, simple, pure. In order to bring out the full potential that so many cooks overlook, at Kitcho every aspect of rice preparation is planned with exquisite care: how long the rice is soaked in cold water, how it is cooked, how to time the finished rice so that it is ready exactly when needed. They say it takes years to be able to make the perfect bowl of rice. It does—years, a practiced eye, and an even more practiced palate.

Dashi Stock: The Heart of Japanese Cooking
In Japanese cookery, *dashi* or soup stock is crucially important. The key to making delicious Japanese food lies in making delicious stock, using ingredients that may include shaved bonito, kelp, small dried fish (usually anchovies) called *niboshi*, and dried shiitake mushroom. While there are many ways of making stock, the combination of kelp and bonito lies at the center of them all. Stock made with this base has innumerable applications in cooking, as it enhances the flavor of any kind of food.

At Kitcho, in addition to kelp-bonito stock, Kunio often uses stock made with kelp alone. Instead of boiling the kelp, he soaks it in cold water for a set length of time, using the resulting stock in dishes where he particularly wants to bring out the natural flavor of ingredients.

There are two kinds of bonito-kelp stock: primary stock (*ichiban dashi*) and secondary stock (*niban dashi*). Primary stock is used mostly for clear soups, where its delicate, refined flavor is indispensable. However, if the bonito flavor of the stock would conflict with the flavor of soup ingredients, simple kelp stock can be used instead. Secondary stock is used in cooking vegetables to give them a more full-bodied flavor. In this book, the term "soup stock" refers generally to secondary stock.

Good soup stock requires not only high-grade ingredients and pure water but careful attention to the cooking process. Below are recipes for basic stock and various related condiment-style sauces. The latter are very useful, as they have a broad range of applications. At Kitcho, stock is made fresh daily.

SOUP STOCKS

Kelp Stock: Rinse 1¾ oz. (50 g) of kelp for *dashi* stock (*dashi kombu*), which are fairly large pieces of kelp. Set in one liter of water and refrigerate for about sixteen hours; if a constant temperature of around 40 °F (5 °C) can be maintained, refrigeration is unnecessary. The results will differ slightly each time, so monitor the flavor and remove the kelp at a suitable time, reserving it to make secondary stock if desired.

Primary Stock: Set one liter of kelp stock over a medium flame, and when it reaches about 175 °F (80 °C), just before boiling, add 1 ⅓ oz. (40 g) of shaved bonito and remove from heat. Approximately 15 seconds after the flakes have sunk to the bottom, strain gently without squeezing. Reserve the flakes to make secondary stock if desired.

Secondary Stock: Place the kelp used for kelp stock in one liter of water over a medium flame; adding another ⅞ oz. (25 g) of new kelp will improve the flavor. When the water comes to a boil, remove the kelp and add the bonito flakes used in making primary stock, along with approximately ¾ oz. (20 g) of fresh flakes. Lower the heat and simmer for about twenty minutes; monitor the taste and turn off the heat when the desired flavor is achieved. Strain immediately.

CONDIMENT-STYLE SAUCES

Salty Stock (*Shio-happo*): One hudred parts secondary stock to two parts salt. Mix the stock and salt in a pan and heat almost to boiling, then cool. Among other applications, this stock is used as a preliminary seasoning for simmered vegetables, where color enhancement is important.

Umami Stock (*Uma-dashi*): Four parts secondary stock, one part soy sauce and one part *mirin* sweet cooking sake, along with kelp (*dashi kombu*) and shaved bonito as desired. Combine stock, *mirin*, and kelp in a saucepan and heat until the alcohol burns off. Then add the soy sauce and shaved bonito and boil for a few seconds before turning off the heat. Strain after cooling. This sauce is excellent with *hiyamugi* noodles, tempura, and so on.

Tosa Vinegar (*Tosa-zu*): Ten parts secondary stock, two and a half parts *mirin* sweet cooking sake, four and a half parts rice vinegar, three parts soy sauce, and kelp and shaved bonito to taste. Combine stock, *mirin*, and kelp in a saucepan and heat until the alcohol burns off. Then add the rice vinegar and bring to a boil. Immediately add the soy sauce, then the shaved bonito; boil for a few seconds, and turn off the heat. Strain after cooling. Tosa vinegar is served with grilled crab as a dipping sauce, and in vinegared dishes such as vinegared crab (*kanisu*), vinegared tilefish, and the like as a dressing.

Tosa Vinegar Gelée: One hundred fifty parts Tosa vinegar, two and a half parts powdered gelatin. Heat the Tosa vinegar in a saucepan and add the powdered gelatin, stirring continuously. When the gelatin has dissolved, remove from heat and allow to cool. For dishes that will sit awhile, this sauce works better than plain Tosa vinegar, as the gelée captures the flavor of the vinegar and prevents it from becoming stronger, allowing greater flexibility in the preparation and serving of some dishes.

Blended Soy-*Dashi* Dipping Sauce (*Wari-joyu*): One part primary stock, one part soy sauce, and kelp and shaved bonito to taste. Combine the kelp and shaved bonito with the soy sauce and leave for one day. Strain and add to the stock. This dipping sauce is used with thinly sliced sashimi and other dishes that would be overwhelmed by the flavor of soy sauce alone.

Chili Citrus Flavoring (*Chiri-zu*): Three parts primary stock, five parts soy sauce, seven parts grated daikon radish, three parts citrus juice, 1 part minced long onion, ground chili pepper. Lightly squeeze the grated radish and mix with the stock, soy sauce, juice, and long onion, then add the chili pepper. This sauce lends a tart flavoring to fish, vegetables, and other foods, and is a good dipping sauce for sashimi.

Food Notes

SPRING CUISINE

March, April, May

SIGNATURE INGREDIENTS FOR SPRING

SEAFOOD
Red ark clam, Venus clam, abalone, sea bream, cuttlefish, whitebait

VEGETABLES
Bamboo shoots, cabbage, snap peas, garland chrysanthemum, rape buds, broad beans, small buds from the Japanese prickly ash (*kinome*)

WILD GREENS
Ostrich fern fiddleheads, plantain lily (*urui*), buds of the angelica tree, *koshiabura* (buds from the slender *Acanthopanax sciadophylloides* tree), horsetail, bracken sprouts, butterbur (*fuki*), udo (a vegetable stalk reminiscent of asparagus)

Pan-Roasted Rice Balls   PAGE 15

SERVING VESSEL: Gilded bamboo husk

These triangular rice balls (*onigiri* in Japanese) are smaller than the standard, and can be consumed in a bite or two. They are made from cooked white rice mixed with finely chopped and seasoned bonito and kelp (*kombu*). Once the rice has been cooked and shaped, each triangle is browned on one side in a frying pan coated with rice bran oil and then sprinkled with grains of toasted rice. The pan-fried side is crunchy, the toasted rice crisp, the rest soft and springy. Thus, with each bite,

three separate textures and subtle taste sensations greet the palate at once—four, if the carefully toasted paper-thin *nori* seaweed is added to the tally. The tradition of wrapping rice cakes in bamboo husks for a lunch goes back to the seventeenth century. Here, the modest husk has been given a luxurious coat of gold paint. The result is a terse elegance in a lavish Rimpa-like style.

*Wild Greens and Red Ark Clam
    with a Tosa Vinegar Gelée*
*Wild Greens with Sesame
    Cream Sauce*   PAGES 16–17

SERVING VESSELS: Ceramic birds and lantern-shaped appetizer dishes, ca. 1960
ARTIST: Hanshichi Shirai

The lids of these small bird-shaped serving vessels lift off to reveal boiled red ark clam (also called blood clam or cockle) and an assortment of lightly seasoned wild greens, notably ostrich fern and *koshiabura*, served with grated ginger and Tosa vinegar gelée (see facing page). On this day, the dish was served in tandem with *Wild Greens with Sesame Cream Sauce*, featuring rape buds (*nanohana*), plantain lily (*urui*), and shiitake mushrooms. The greens were parboiled and lightly seasoned with Kitcho's salty stock (see facing page) while the shiitake was lightly salted and grilled. The vegetables were then dressed with a creamy white sesame sauce. In Japan, flavorful wild greens such as these herald the arrival of spring. Served in a lantern-shaped vessel.

Assorted Sashimi in Flowing Water   PAGES 20–21

SERVING VESSEL: Rectangular Bizen dish, ca. 1930
ARTIST: Rosanjin Kitaoji

This stoneware dish, fired in the austere Bizen style much cherished in Japan, was made from the rich chocolate-hued clay of the region. Glistening with water, the platter is filled with an assortment of delicacies: extra fatty bluefin tuna, red sea bream (a special springtime treat), and squid (here, the common European cuttlefish, known in Japanese as *mongo-ika*).

For decoration, white threads of shredded daikon radish garnish the platter, lending a poetic touch to the presentation with their suggestion of swirling water or waves. The radish is pared in long, exceedingly thin bands that are wound in spirals. Three other garnishes add discrete splashes of color: a variety of mustard green (*mizuna* in Japanese), julienned Japanese pumpkin, and high-quality wasabi. Bits of gold foil provide a touch of playfulness and a counterpoint to the dark-hued plate.

Two other culinary techniques are employed in making sashimi. The first is precision slicing of the fish to bring out the full flavor. To accomplish this, skill with the knife is paramount: angles must be precise, the sliced surface glossy upon finishing. An additional bit of finesse is required for sea bream. The umami flavor of this fish lies just under the skin, which is therefore left in place. Dousing the fish briefly with hot water whitens the surface as if it's been touched by a light frost—hence the Japanese name for this technique, *shimofuri*, or falling frost—after which the skin is scored in a diagonal crosshatch pattern.

Over and above the aesthetic effect, this blanching technique has many advantages, removing fishy odors as well as any fat or impurities on the surface. It softens the skin to a delectable texture and coaxes out a full-bodied umami flavor that cannot be tasted when sea bream is eaten raw. This treatment also makes it possible to enjoy variations in texture: the silky smoothness of the skin, the tender outer surface, and the firmer center.

Clear Chicken Kelp Soup PAGE 22

SERVING VESSEL: Lacquer soup bowl with cherry blossoms in mother-of-pearl inlay, ca. 1970

In Japanese cuisine, clear soup is generally made with clams or other seafood, or the head of a large fish such as sea bream, but here chicken is used instead. Wings with skin and bones intact are smothered in salt and left to sit for ten minutes, then rinsed in hot water and patted dry. Ten minutes of simmering in kelp stock and the chicken broth is done. It is seasoned with small amounts of salt, pepper, and soy sauce. Ingredients include salted thigh meat grilled to a golden brown and cut into bite-size morsels; shredded spring onion; finely chopped aromatic sprigs and small buds from the Japanese prickly ash (*kinome*); and, for additional aroma, grilled spring onion. There is no chicken smell. This wholesome soup has a deeply satisfying flavor.

Venus Clam Soup PAGE 23

SERVING VESSELS: Lacquer soup bowls decorated with plum blossoms and Japanese bush warblers, ca. 1970

Raw Venus clams are sliced crosswise in half, and the firm "tongue" scored. The clams are then marinated in kelp stock and removed. The remaining stock is simmered with a bit of salt and soy sauce, and the clam meat returned at the last moment. Sesame tofu is placed in the center

of the bowl and topped with the sliced clams sprinkled with pepper. Fragrant garnishes include slivered *udo*, a Japanese herb in the ginseng family reminiscent of asparagus; young leaves of Japanese prickly ash (*kinome*); and lightly grilled dried sea cucumber roe (*konoko*). Pungent flavors of the seashore—kelp, clam, *konoko*—blend perfectly with the woodland herbs. The soup bowl is lavishly decorated with *maki-e* (patterns drawn in lacquerware and sprinkled with gold powder), even on the foot, which is normally unseen.

DOLL FESTIVAL SPECIALS: Goby and Egg Scramble and Assorted Spring Vegetables PAGE 24

SERVING VESSELS: Ceramic husband-and-wife *hina* doll dishes with removable lids, ca. 1935
ARTIST: Kahei Shima

On March 3, Japanese families celebrate a daughter's growth and wish for her continued health and happiness by setting out special figurines called *hina* dolls, along with colored rice dumplings, peach blossoms, and *amazake*, a traditional hot drink made from fermented rice. At Kitcho, the Doll Festival is marked by displaying a pair of standing antique *hina* dolls. During the meal one dish is presented that has special visual appeal and a gentle flavor suited to the occasion. The dish at left combines small pieces of goby fish with a Japanese egg scramble called *tamago toji*, while the other offers an assortment of carefully prepared delicacies—horsetail and ostrich fern, shiitake mushroom and Chinese yam, Rikyu-fu wheat gluten (see *Moon and Pampas Grass Tray*, page 180), rape buds—matched with a refreshing Tosa vinegar gelée flavored with pickled-apricot paste (*bainiku*).

Hassun Appetizers à la Rimpa, with Decorated Shells PAGES 26–27

SERVING VESSELS: Lacquer tray with decorative rail, ca. 1970; real and ceramic shells

This tray offers a cornucopia of spring favorites at their peak. Spring, when trees put out new shoots, is also the season of shellfish: Venus and littleneck clam, red ark clam, and

more. Here, instead of focusing on shellfish cuisine per se, Kunio uses shells as serving vessels for other foods in a colorful and eye-catching display. Blue-and-white porcelain cups in the shape of turban shellsfish share pride of place with actual scallop and clam shells decorated with gold foil in Rimpa-like patterns. The shells hold a festive array of foods and flavors: bright simmered tiger shrimp, tender beef tongue and abalone, sweet egg custard (*tamagoyaki*) cut to resemble slices of sponge cake, and morsels of red ark clam with shallots and tasty horsetail shoots (*tsukushi*) in a vinegared miso dressing. The display evokes spring in all its glory.

Steamed Custard with Two Cheeses PAGE 28

SERVING VESSELS: Small lidded porcelain cups with overglaze enamel, ca. 1915
ARTIST: Eiraku Myozen

At Kitcho, the basic recipe for the classic Japanese steamed custard known as *chawanmushi* uses 1 cup (225 cc) of *dashi* stock for each egg, and is seasoned with salt and soy sauce. Traditionally, other ingredients include plump steamed shrimp, lily bulb, ginkgo nuts, and *matsutake* mushroom; but Kunio's recipe calls for soft Castelo Branco cheese and a rich topping of grated parmesan. This contemporary twist on a time-honored dish offers not only the luscious abundance of two savory cheeses, but also a pleasant jolt of surprise: most Japanese diners would never expect to find cheese, an unconventional ingredient, in such a familiar setting.

Blossom-Viewing Picnic Lunch PAGE 33

SERVING VESSELS: Stacked lacquer trays (*jubako*) with gold-leaf decoration (*maki-e*), ca. 1970

When cherry blossom season arrives and the very air is suffused with flowering clouds of

pale pink, orders come in for blossom-viewing picnic lunches. So popular is this activity that at the height of the season Kitcho is likely to include small picnic boxes with the meal, so that diners can imagine themselves feasting outdoors as they gaze into the garden or enjoy a room decorated for the arrival of spring. Of the four compartments in this elegant lacquered container, one holds *Scattered Sushi* (*chirashi-zushi* in Japanese), in which ingredients spill artfully across a bed of vinegared rice. The other three are packed with a rich variety of spring delicacies: lightly grilled scallop ligaments, red ark clam sashimi, salmon roe, sweet Japanese pumpkin, lotus root, wild greens (angelica tree shoots, bracken sprouts, plantain lily, butterbur), and more. The result is a delightful picnic meal filled with the bounty of mountain and sea and a rainbow of bright colors.

Beef and Vegetable Sushi   PAGE 35

SERVING VESSEL: "Cherry-Petal Storm" plate by Kunio Tokuoka and Okura Art China, 2008

In this dish, created with spring in mind, Kunio gives sushi an innovative twist. The standard topping of sliced tuna or other seafood is replaced with a heartier one: thinly sliced beef, lightly seared at the edges (*tataki*, in Japanese) and sprinkled with Japanese mustard. Normally for mixed sushi, vinegared rice would be mixed with chopped dried shiitake (softened in cold water) and burdock, both simmered in sugar and soy sauce. But here, stir-fried minced onion and shiitake are mixed in to support the rich flavor of the meat, along with finely chopped bits from the edge of the *tataki* and wild greens: shoots of the angelica tree (*taranome*), Japanese prickly ash, butterbur, and bracken (*warabi*). Accompanying this flavor-rich sushi is a more austere—yet no less flavorful—cooked salad of grilled bamboo shoots and rape buds (*nanohana*), two symbols of spring. The salad is dressed with a mixture of Japanese

mustard, vinegar, and miso, and then topped with garlic chips. The perfectly matched food and vessel exemplify Kunio's creative vision.

Mélange of Spring Greens   PAGE 36

SERVING VESSEL: Jingdezhen porcelain bowl, late Ming Dynasty, China.

Kunio's grandfather Teiichi used to use this very bowl to serve late-fall taro (*satoimo*) simmered with abalone and sprinkled with an abundance of Japanese citron (*yuzu*) zest. Here, the Ming-dynasty treasure has been drafted to showcase a wealth of tender spring vegetables. Soft spring cabbage, sweet snap peas, bracken with its bitter tinge and characteristic slipperiness, long onion, and Japanese pumpkin are all simmered separately in kelp stock with salt and butter. Each type of vegetable is cooked individually to heighten the seasonal flavor and prevent a mingling, and muddling, of tastes. The deep-fried food is Venus clam. For an interesting texture and flavor accent, the clam is coated with crushed crackers known as *kakinotane*, literally "persimmon seeds": little rice crackers shaped to resemble seeds and coated with a spicy mix of soy sauce, chili, and other flavorings. The sauce is made by cooking daikon radish and long onion in kelp stock, salt, and butter, then puréeing the vegetables in a blender until thick and creamy. A mound of finely julienned cabbage, sprinkled with ground chili pepper, garnishes the center. The vibrant natural colors of the spring foods are well set off by the elegant yet subdued coloring of this splendid bowl, with its twisting floral segments and beautiful cobalt hue.

Bamboo Shoot Mélange   PAGE 39

SERVING VESSEL: Large hand-painted bowl with cherry blossom and maple leaf designs, ca. 1930
ARTIST: Rosanjin Kitaoji

Here fresh, crisp bamboo shoot, a representative spring vegetable, is prepared in three tempting ways. The shoots are first parboiled to make them tender, after which they are either simmered in a seasoned kelp stock, grilled in a sweet sauce with soy sauce and sweetened cooking sake (*mirin*) after simmering, or coated with batter and

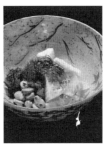

deep-fried *tempura* style. While the main ingredient remains the same, the different cooking methods offer a range of delicious tones and textures. A generous handful of grilled broad beans topped with *kinome* (sprigs and tender leaf buds of the Japanese prickly ash) complements the bamboo shoots perfectly. The design of this bowl is auspicious, featuring cherry blossoms and fall leaves, emblems of different seasons that together represent time's endless stream. Food in the bowl is arranged so that the cherry blossoms are prominent in the spring, and in the fall, the bright leaves stand out. For the fall, the bowl is sometimes filled with mouth-watering grilled shrimp taro, a locally grown variety of taro.

Whole Grilled Bamboo Shoots   PAGES 40–41

This charmingly rustic, seemingly *in situ* presentation of bamboo shoots gives the impression of freshly dug shoots cooked on the spot in a bamboo grove. Grilling a bamboo shoot in the husk intensifies its natural sweetness, goodness, and slight astringency, allowing a full appreciation of the delicate, woodsy flavor and crisp yet tender texture.

Japanese Risotto   PAGE 42

SERVING VESSEL: Red Raku ware pot, ca. 1970
ARTIST: Masatake Fukumori

How should one cook rice in kelp stock? Should it be simmered in stock made by soaking kelp in cold water and then removing it and adding bonito shavings—or might it be

better to cook the rice in kelp stock alone and add bonito shavings at the very end? Such considerations lie behind this innovative dish, which takes the latter approach, giving the flavor of the rice an unexpected purity. Kunio cooks the rice risotto-style, first sautéing it in olive oil and then cooking it *al dente* with frequent additions of kelp stock. He tops it with finely chopped kelp simmered in soy sauce and *mirin*; crumbled bonito that has been soaked in soy sauce and dried; and minced rape buds that have been boiled and marinated in salted kelp stock. A loose scattering of dried bonito shavings provides the final touch.

Rice Topped with Egg and Tempura   PAGE 43

SERVING VESSEL: Black earthenware pot, 2009
ARTIST: Masatake Fukumori

At Kitcho, this dish is prepared in a *donabe*, a thick-bodied clay cooking pot with matching lid. The pot is glazed and decorated so the food can be served as-is, nestled in its clay bed. First, rice is cooked in kelp stock flavored with salt and light soy sauce. The rice mixture is then covered and brought to a boil, after which tiny raw whitebait (not pictured) are placed across the top in a single layer and the pot is covered again. After fifteen minutes, the fish and rice are topped with thin omelet ribbons, whitebait tempura, and finely chopped aromatic buds from the Japanese prickly ash (*kinome*). The cover is once again replaced and the rice is served. This colorful dish offers an incredible variety of flavors and textures, mixing the melt-in-your-mouth texture and delicate taste of plump steamed whitebait with the aroma, goodness, and crispness of whitebait tempura, along with the tender steamed omelet strips and moist, short-grained rice. The inspired addition of tempura-fried whitebait lends this dish a special appeal. Made in a quantity sufficient to serve 6 to 8 people.

Sea Bream Chazuke   PAGE 43

SERVING VESSEL: Lacquer bowl with silver and gold, replica of a piece by Rosanjin Kitaoji, ca. 1955

Chazuke is a quick simple meal that consists of rice and toppings with hot tea poured over. *Sea Bream Chazuke* is an important dish at

Kitcho. The name of the restaurant Teiichi Yuki founded in 1930 was in fact "Ontaicha-dokoro Kitcho," or "Sea Bream and Tea Kitcho." The original dish as prepared by Teiichi featured slices of sea bream sashimi marinated in soy sauce, sake, and sweetened cooking sake, then mixed with sesame paste and served on white rice submerged in brewed green tea. In Kunio's version, the tea—which is lightly salted for flavor—is not added right away. First, a slice of unmarinated sea bream sashimi is topped with dollops of sesame sauce and eaten mixed with rice, *nori*, and *wasabi*. Finally, after consuming several slices of sashimi in this fashion, the diner pours the steaming green tea over the remaining rice. This is another delicious way of enjoying this simple yet classic dish.

Japanese Confections   PAGE 44

SERVING VESSELS: Two small lacquer plates; Dutch porcelain dish

These three traditional Japanese sweets (known collectively as *wagashi*) were made with spring in mind. The confection on top, called *Cherry Blossom Rice Dumpling*, or *Sakura-mochi*, consists of a sweet pink rice dough filled with smooth red bean jam, wrapped in a pickled cherry leaf. In the center is *Bracken Dumpling*, or *Warabi-mochi*, a jelly-like confection made from bracken starch and sprinkled with toasted soybean flour (*kinako*); it is sweetened with a very un-Japanese ingredient: powdered maple sugar. At the bottom is *Green Tea Tiramisu with Mascarpone*. At Kitcho, confections are made by hand daily, always keeping the season and seasonal events in mind.

Skewered Delicacies   PAGES 46–47

SERVING VESSELS: Decorated cylindrical appetizer vessels, eighteenth century
ARTIST: Rimpa artist Ogata Kenzan

This type of deep cylindrical vessel is traditionally used for the winter tea cere-

mony. Regardless of the season, Kitcho founder Teiichi would sometimes serve shrimp and octopus on thin, short strips of bamboo inserted in these Ogata Kenzan dishes. Kunio's version is a more playful take on his grandfather's innovation. Skewering tender bites of shrimp, sweet potato, okra, and gingko-nut dumplings on long, thin strips of bamboo, Kunio brings a playful sensibility to the table, letting the bamboo skewers hang and sway like stalks of ripe grass.

SUMMER CUISINE
June, July, August

SIGNATURE INGREDIENTS FOR SUMMER
SEAFOOD Pike conger, marbled sole, octopus, eel, horse mackerel, sweetfish, abalone
VEGETABLES Young lotus root, okra, Japanese pumpkin, eggplant, Kamo eggplant (a Kyoto variety), Fushimi-togarashi mild pepper (a Kyoto variety), water shield leaf, myoga ginger, perilla leaf (also called beefsteak plant or Japanese basil)

Hot Blanched Pike Conger   PAGE 51

SERVING VESSELS: Square blue-and-white porcelain bowls with wheat-straw pattern, ca. 1895
ARTIST: Eiraku Tokuzen, fourteenth-generation potter

Pike conger, the long eel-like fish known in Japanese as *hamo*, is a favorite of Kyotoites. Its preparation is complicated by its myriad tiny bones, too numerous to be removed. Instead, the fish is prepared in a culinary *tour de force* requiring the chef to create innumerable fine cuts that score through flesh and bone while leaving the skin intact. Then the fish is chopped into inch-wide pieces, dredged in kudzu starch. After being blanched in lightly salted boiling kelp stock just long enough to soften the skin, the pieces are transferred to lidded containers to be eaten while hot. Bright dabs of tangy pickled-apricot paste (*bainiku*), mixed with minced ginger pickled in sweetened vinegar, go beautifully with pike conger. A bit of hot boiled mustard green (*mizuna*) adds extra color and texture. Served with blended soy-*dashi* dipping sauce (page 172).

The drama of this dish lies in the moment when the lid comes off, releasing a cloud of fragrant steam. As blanched pike conger is usually plunged straight into ice water and served chilled, Kunio's presentation, which brings out the full natural umami of the skin, comes as a delightful surprise.

Basket of Hassun Morsels PAGE 52

SERVING VESSELS: Crystal sake cups by Baccarat, ca. 1920; bamboo basket by Hiki Ikkan, nineteenth century

For this refreshing and elegant summer repast, assorted delicacies are arranged on a bed of crushed ice in an antique basket made of finely woven bamboo. The morsels of food are served in petite, yet elegant, sake cups of Baccarat crystal; the remaining decorations comprise cuttings of fresh green mulberry leaves, brightly colored Chinese-lantern pods, and purple clematis. In a kaiseki meal, the *hassun* course establishes the seasonal theme with an assortment of foods at their absolute peak. The crystal sake cups hold tiny bits of octopus, boiled Japanese pumpkin, garland chrysanthemum greens, and minced lettuce. Inside the Chinese lantern pods are sweet simmered *gori* fish. Arranged on the mulberry leaves are Japanese bayberries marinated in liqueur, simmered *kinugasa* mushrooms stuffed with

pounded okra and topped with pickled-apricot paste (*bainiku*), smoked salmon, and lightly sweetened simmered broad beans.

Marbled Sole Sashimi PAGE 56

SERVING VESSEL: Jingdezhen ware platter with decoration in blue underglaze, Ming Dynasty, China

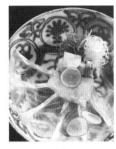

This marbled sole sashimi is sliced to a translucent thinness, allowing the underlying design on the blue-and-white Ming platter to show through. The arrangement is meant to suggest white peony petals. Although Kunio takes pride in the beauty of this traditional presentation, he stresses that for sashimi, extreme thinness is never the goal per se. Texture, a key element in flavor, requires a certain thickness which varies with the type and size of fish used. In the center of the platter are the high-fat, richly flavorful flesh near the fins, and the liver, garnished with green and white shredded onion and wasabi. The liver may be eaten dipped in blended soy-*dashi* sauce or citron vinegar (*kankitsu-su*), or wrapped in a slice of sashimi, according to taste.

Cold Turtle Soup PAGE 58

SERVING VESSELS: Small crystal bowls by Baccarat, ca. 1920

This golden soup is made by slowly simmering soft-shell turtle meat. The dark squares are tender, gelatinous turtle from the outer edges of the body, the orange orbs are turtle eggs, and the green balls are made of pounded okra. Finely sliced onion and a touch of ginger juice garnish the soup, which is at once savory and elegant. Every drop contains the exceptional umami of the turtle, a full-bodied flavor that seeps into the marrow of your bones.

Shrimp, Grilled Shiitake, and Water Shield Leaf in Tosa Vinegar PAGE 61

SERVING VESSELS: Silver plates; small crystal bowls by Baccarat, ca. 1920

Seared shrimp, grilled shiitake mushrooms and lotus root, boiled okra and lily bulb, and water shield leaf are served in refreshing Tosa vinegar (page 172). The miscanthus reed rings (*chinowa*) that encircle the silver plates are an allusion to an ancient midyear purification ceremony observed in Kyoto on the last day of June.

Octopus Triad PAGE 63

SERVING VESSEL: Ice balloon

A globe of ice lined with cucumber leaves serves as a vessel for morsels of octopus prepared in three distinct ways. The round tidbits are deep-fried suction cups spiced with a coating of crushed "persimmon seed" rice crackers. The slices garnished with tangy pickled-apricot paste (*bainiku*) were salted and plunged swiftly first into boiling water, then ice water. The remaining pieces were coated with rice bran oil and lightly sautéed. Nestled with the octopus are various seasonal vegetables: blanched asparagus, grilled fresh shiitake mushrooms, simmered *hasuimo* taro stalks with light seasoning, and yellow zucchini.

Grilled Summer Vegetables PAGE 65

SERVING VESSEL: Square crystal dish by Baccarat, ca. 1935

Each ingredient in this medley of summer vegetables is brushed with rice bran oil (except the eggplant) and lightly grilled to bring out its deepest flavor. Okra and the long green pepper

called Fushimi-togarashi—traditional Kyoto vegetables—are cut in bite-sized pieces after grilling, while lotus root and Japanese pumpkin are first steamed and cut up, then pan-fried on one side. Eggplant is grilled with the skin on, then peeled and cut into pieces. The vegetables are seasoned with umami stock thinned with secondary stock, then garnished with finely sliced myoga ginger. Just before eating, dried shaved bonito flakes are sprinkled on top (not shown).

Depending on the menu, Kitcho uses olive oil, sesame oil, and various other cooking oils. Rice bran oil, used here, provides sheen and delicate flavor without any added aroma.

Eggplant and Baby Red Shrimp   PAGE 66

SERVING VESSEL: Blue-and-white oblong porcelain bowl, nineteenth century
ARTIST: Eiraku Hozen, eleventh-generation potter

Kamo eggplant, another summer vegetable cultivated in Kyoto, is round and lustrous, with dense, richly flavorful flesh. It's prepared in this dish by removing the calyx and peel, and then, without any coating of flour or batter, deep-frying just long enough for the oil to penetrate the surface. The dried shrimp are also deep-fried to a savory crisp. The eggplant is braised in *dashi* soup stock mixed with sweet cooking sake and soy sauce till tender, then arranged alongside the shrimp with a generous mound of finely sliced green onion on top. The melt-in-your-mouth eggplant and crisp, crunchy shrimp make a superb contrast in texture and color.

Cabbage and Horse Mackerel Mille-Feuille   PAGE 66

SERVING VESSEL: Black lacquer tray

Cabbage leaves are first softened in salt and then marinated in kelp stock before being layered with mackerel sashimi. The resulting mille-feuille is refrigerated for an hour or so to allow the flavors to blend, then cut into portions, arranged on serving vessels, and garnished with perilla buds and finely shredded ginger. It is dressed with a Tosa vinegar gelée (see page 172). The sweetness and freshness of the cabbage sets off the oil-rich flesh of the mackerel beautifully.

Grilled Eel Uzaku   PAGE 67

SERVING VESSELS: Oblong crystal cut glass dishes, Baccarat replicas

Summer's debilitating heat calls for a nourishing, tasty dish of grilled eel, the traditional cure for summer fatigue. *Uzaku* is usually a kind of grilled eel-and-cucumber vinaigrette, the bite-sized pieces dressed in "three-flavored vinegar"—in Japanese, *sanbaizu*—containing vinegar, soy sauce, and sweet cooking sake (*mirin*). Here, generous portions consisting of half an eel have instead been broiled with the same thick, sweet sauce used for *kabayaki*, another popular grilled eel dish. Instead of cucumber, Kunio uses shredded cabbage, slivered myoga ginger, ginger, and perilla leaves, all rubbed lightly with salt and cured in kelp stock, as an accompaniment. These are topped with a decorative flavor accent of ginger triangles marinated in sweetened vinegar.

Salt-Grilled Sweetfish   PAGES 70–71

SERVING VESSEL: Bamboo basket in the shape used for traditional cormorant fishing

Ayu, or sweetfish, are also known in Japanese as *kogyo*, "fragrant fish"; as the name indicates, their fragrance is integral to their flavor. To bring out the wonderful aroma, live fish are skewered and salted, then slowly grilled to perfection. By midsummer, sweetfish are approximately 6 inches (15 cm) long, with tender bones. Grilling over a low flame further softens the bones so that the fish can be eaten whole, even the head and tail. For guests who prefer their fish boneless, a server will remove the bones without altering the shape of the fish.

Sea Urchin Grilled in a Kelp Boat   PAGE 72

SERVING VESSEL: Pure silver mesh basket

A boat-shaped container fashioned from kelp is heaped with raw sea urchin and grilled over a charcoal fire. Raw sea urchin is beautiful to begin with, and here it acquires a fine kelp flavoring and a thick, creamy texture that make it truly exceptional. The harmony of sea urchin and kelp flavors is outstanding. The topping consists of minced kelp.

Abalone Sashimi   PAGE 73

SERVING VESSEL: Cut crystal dish, ca. 1945

Dashi soup stock, made using primary stock and abalone *engawa*, is lightly salted and heated to 140 °F (60 °C). Thin, translucent slices of abalone are swished in the stock *shabu-shabu* style, then spread on a bed of finely chopped lettuce that has been gently cooked in the same stock. The sashimi is served with dabs of pale-green wasabi, radish circles, tiny cubes of boiled pumpkin, and frozen balls of abalone liver sauce. The latter is made by boiling the liver with salt and straining it, blending in primary stock and soy sauce, and freezing. To eat, wasabi, liver sauce, and lettuce are wrapped in a sashimi slice, dipped in the stock, and enjoyed in a single mouthful. The symphonic blend of flavors is at once deeply satisfying and refreshing.

Grilled Abalone Isoyaki   PAGE 74

It's a bit difficult to make out in the photograph, but outside the abalone shell is green *nori* seaweed which, when heated, releases the aroma of the seaside. Inside the shell, on a layer of savory tofu-like egg custard, are sautéed abalone slices, shiitake mushrooms, and stalks of trefoil, topped with needles

of *udo* (a vegetable stalk reminiscent of asparagus). Lightly seasoned primary stock is then poured over all, and the concoction is simmered over a portable charcoal burner. The final touch is a sprinkling of grated Japanese citron (*yuzu*) peel. The seaside smells of abalone and *nori* mingle enticingly with the earthy smells of citron, trefoil, and *udo*.

Lotus Flower Hassun, Kitcho Version   PAGE 75

At Obon, the midsummer Buddhist festival honoring departed ancestors, it is traditional to decorate one's house with lotus flowers and set out food offerings on lotus leaves for returning spirits. Because they rise above the mud to bloom, lotus flowers are an important symbol in the Buddhist tradition, representing the human capacity to attain enlightenment; Buddhist statues often depict their subjects seated on a lotus flower. Here, a lotus leaf serves as a large serving dish, and pink petals as dainty containers for *hijiki* seaweed, sweet potato, beef tongue, raw sea urchin, and shrimp. This simple yet elegant dish is a Kitcho tradition begun by founder Teiichi.

Lotus Flower Hassun, Kunio Version   PAGES 76–77

SERVING VESSELS: Silver platter ca. 1935; crystal sake cups by Baccarat, ca. 1920; small oblong blue dish

Nestled in the lotus petals is a bit of savory chicken skin, simmered in sweetened soy sauce and mixed with finely sliced celery; nearby on the small leaf are shrimp simmered in lightly sweetened broth and sweet potato circles simmered to a faint sweetness. The Baccarat sake cups contain fresh sea urchin, grilled abalone, and boiled garland chrysanthemum greens. Lotus petals are scattered to recreate the natural beauty of fallen petals.

Sweetfish Rice   PAGE 78

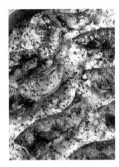

Sweetfish—*ayu* in Japanese—are grilled and then filleted, the bones set to simmer in kelp stock which is then used to cook the rice, adding depth of flavor. When the stock comes to a boil, the rice is topped with the sweetfish. A generous dusting of minced water pepper, or *tade*, a pungent Japanese herb that goes particularly well with sweetfish, completes the presentation.

Lotus Rice   PAGE 79

SERVING VESSELS: Round wooden steamer; circular wooden trays
ARTIST: Trays by Hikobei Nishimura

The rice is cooked in an earthenware pot, the water replaced with secondary stock. The lotus root is first steamed, then cut into assorted small shapes and sautéed in rice bran oil just long enough to brown the corners. Just before the rice is done, it is topped with the lotus root, covered, and allowed to steam a bit more. The mixture is transferred to the wooden steamers and topped with a colorful medley of dried and lightly salted baby sardines (*chirimenjako*), toasted white sesame seeds, pickled-apricot paste (*bainiku*), and chiffonaded perilla leaves. The dish should be served piping hot; diners mix the ingredients slightly before falling to. The tart pickled apricot, salty *chirimenjako*, sweet lotus root and rice, savory toasted sesame, and piquant perilla leaf make for a veritable symphony of flavors and textures.

Cold Summer Noodles Set in Bamboo   PAGE 79

Coiled inside a segment of green bamboo are wheat-flour noodles called *hiyamugi*, which are just a bit thicker than *somen*, the quintessential cold noodles of summer in Japan. Shrimp and a slice of dried shiitake mushroom simmered in sweetened soy sauce; several dabs of boiled, pounded okra; and a soft-boiled egg yolk round out this refreshing dish. The yolk is cooked by boiling a small egg for twenty minutes at 150°–155 °F (65°–68 °C), then chilling it in cold water; since the white and the yolk harden at different temperatures, the white comes out jellied, the yolk soft-boiled. This is known in Japan as a "hot-spring egg," or *onsen tamago*.

Before eating, the bamboo is lifted, releasing the noodles and other ingredients to steep in the broth underneath. This dish was a big hit at the Osaka World Expo in 1970.

Japanese Shaved Ice with Green Tea Syrup and Bean Jam   PAGE 83

SERVING VESSEL: Replica of classic Totoya-style tea bowl
ARTIST: Shojiro Yuki of Tokyo Kitcho

The shaved ice contains tender dumplings made of glutinous rice flour and red bean paste with whole adzuki beans. The mildly sweet syrup is made with thick green tea. The light astringency of green tea and the sweetness of the bean paste, the cool slipperiness of the dumplings, and the chill of ice shavings that quickly melt in the mouth all combine to make a dessert in the classic Japanese style—the perfect way to cool off on a hot summer day.

FALL CUISINE

September, October, November

Moon and Pampas Grass Tray — PAGE 87

SERVING VESSEL: Ceramic dish with autumn grass motif, in the style of Ogata Kenzan, ca. 1920
ARTIST: Eiraku Shozen, fifteenth-generation potter

The chopsticks rest on a bit of *susuki*, or pampas grass, atop a "half-moon tray" that looks, to the Western eye, at once chic yet traditional. The bowl bears a design of bellflowers—like pampas, one of the traditional "seven grasses of autumn"—and the flat silver "plate" represents the moon. All in all, an elegant way to celebrate the bright full moon of autumn. Steamed blue swimmer crab is accompanied by boiled, mashed okra; twin orange-colored orbs with the texture of custard cream, made from egg yolk and secondary stock; and simmered "Rikyu-fu" (after tea master Sen no Rikyu), which is wheat gluten boiled in a spicy broth and then deep-fried. Garnished with slivers of chestnut and flavored with Tosa vinegar gelée.

Sirloin in Special Sauce — PAGE 90

SERVING VESSEL: "Seat of the Moon" plate by Kunio Tokuoka and Okura Art China, 2008

The sirloin is cooked in sake in a pressure cooker and served with Kunio's special sauce: red wine, brandy, chicken stock, and

beef shank soup are heated individually until thick and then blended together with *mirin* and soy sauce and heated until the sauce thickens. The mashed potatoes underneath are meltingly soft and smooth. Accompanying these are grilled Fushimi-togarashi, a long green pepper cultivated in Kyoto, and unpeeled slices of steamed sweet potato, browned on one side. Further flavor enhancers—dollops of mustard and a sauce made from garland chrysanthemum sprinkled with ground chili pepper—are set alongside.

Shark Fin Turtle Soup — PAGE 92

SERVING VESSELS: Lacquer bowls decorated with powdered gold leaf (*maki-e*), the underside of each lid showing the moon in a different phase half-hidden behind wispy clouds.
ARTIST: Shuetsu Nakagawa

The broth is turtle soup made with fine sake. Soft, savory tofu-like egg custard is topped with grilled shark fin that was simmered slowly in chicken stock before being lightly browned on one side. The soup is seasoned with ginger juice and garnished with two colors of onion. This is a dish of supreme luxury, an umami-rich harmony of flavors that is immensely satisfying.

Sea Bream and Turnip Hot Pot — PAGES 94–95

SERVING VESSEL: Black earthenware pot, ca. 2000
ARTIST: Masatake Fukumori

This marvelous fall hot pot features a succulent sea bream (*tai*) flanked by turnips whose sweet, nutty flavor is brought on by the onset of cool weather. The two flavors complement each other perfectly. The fish is cooked quickly over high heat in a lightly seasoned soup made of kelp stock boiled with the bony parts of another whole fish. The

turnips, meanwhile, are simmered to tenderness in a broth flavored with turnip parings reduced in kelp stock. Finally the cooked turnips and sea bream are combined, and the seasonings adjusted to taste. Why not cook the actual fish and vegetables together? It's all in the timing: one cooks faster than the other, so if you waited until the turnips were tender, the fish would be ruined. Managing the two separately, Kunio creates another unforgettable gustatory masterpiece.

Roast Shrimp Taro amid Fallen Leaves — PAGE 97

When persimmon, maple, and zelkova leaves changed color and began falling, people used to rake them into piles and make bonfires, tossing on potatoes to roast. In times past, everyone looked forward to such pleasurable events in the fall, but it seems those days are gone. This dish brings back long-ago autumn days through the colors of fallen leaves, the tang of smoke, and the flavor of fluffy, hot shrimp taros steamed and roasted in their jackets. Shrimp taro (*ebi-imo*), a root so named for the shrimp-like stripes on its skin, is a traditional Kyoto vegetable.

Shrimp Taro Croquette — PAGE 97

SERVING VESSEL: Enameled porcelain appetizer dish with white chrysanthemum and floral arabesque motifs, ca. 1950
ARTIST: Eiraku Sokuzen, sixteenth-generation potter

Though Japanese croquettes are generally potato-based, this one is made not with ordinary potato but with shrimp taro, one of Kyoto's traditional vegetables. The mild sweetness of the steamed, sieved taro melts on the tongue. Nestled alongside are grilled sword beans (*nata mame*, properly known as *morokko ingen*); simmered, lightly seasoned Kyoto carrot; and shiitake mushroom. The

pale-green garnish is thinly sliced lettuce sprinkled with ground chili powder. To bring out the delicate flavor of the shrimp taro, Kunio makes a special sauce (*so-fumi*, page 164), first simmering white onion and daikon radish in kelp stock, salt, and butter, then puréeing them in a blender until creamy.

Flower-Screen Hassun   PAGES 100–101

SERVING VESSELS AND ARTISTS: Green leaf-shaped ceramic dishes; blue-and-white ceramic incense containers in the shape of bellflowers by Chikushun Kawase, ca. 1950; ceramic house-shaped vessel with vine motif by Hanshichi Shirai, ca. 1950; lacquered serving tray by Shogoro Konishi, ca. 1970

At Kitcho, the seasons are celebrated with panache. On this *hassun* tray, fall wildflowers and grasses—pinks, gentians, bellflowers, pampas, and *mizuhiki* grass—are set in green bamboo cylinders connected by thin bamboo strips to suggest a living flower screen. To make the lovely lanterns that give off warm and magical light, wide, thin sheets of daikon radish are sliced off with a broad cutting blade, *katsuramuki*-style, and the edges are glued together. For an extra touch of elegance, the upper portions are tinged a faint pink. The fare includes salmon roe marinated in secondary stock and soy sauce, roasted chestnuts, simmered shrimp, grilled sea bream fillets wrapped in *nori* seaweed, and steamed blue swimmer crab in a Tosa vinegar gelée. Inside the lidded incense container is fried *gori* (a rare river fish) with a sweet sauce. In the house-shaped container is tender beef tongue simmered in soy sauce and *mirin*.

Steamed Yuba Wrap   PAGE 102

SERVING VESSEL: Lidded bowl, Oribe ware, ca. 1930

This recipe is a Kunio original. First, he fries bite-sized pieces of Chinese yam while

chunks of salt-water eel (*anago*) grilled in light soy-based sweet sauce. He then wraps the yam and eel morsels in steamed *yuba*, or soymilk skin. After that, he slathers the bundle with *an* (*dashi* stock seasoned with soy sauce and *mirin* and thickened with kudzu flour) and tops it with a ball of finely minced ginger and green onion. The delectable softness of yuba is enhanced by the aroma, textures, and flavors of fried yam and eel. The diminutive bowl used as container for this gentle and enticing concoction fits comfortably inside a woman's palm. This is a dish that soothes body and soul.

Persimmon Vinaigrette   PAGE 103

SERVING VESSEL: Cylindrical appetizer dishes, Oribe ware, ca. 1930
ARTIST: Rosanjin Kitaoji

A variegated feast including pink shrimp, lightly grilled; fresh, milk-white daikon radish; red boiled carrot; pale orange persimmon; green Japanese cucumber; and a jet-black strip of *suizenji nori* seaweed. All but the shrimp are cut in uniform ¾-inch (2-cm) lengths, and a refreshing Tosa vinegar gelée is added to bind the different flavors together. Although it is not clear from the photograph, this vessel is 4 inches (10 cm) deep. Unable to see what the cup holds from a seated position, the diner will instinctively reach to draw it closer and look inside. Such brief moments of drama are part of the pleasure of using these vessels.

Genji Inkstone Lid Hassun   PAGES 104–105

SERVING VESSEL: Inkstone lid with *maki-e* illustration

An assortment of superlative delicacies is artfully arranged to accent the luxurious gold-leaf illustration (*maki-e*) from the tenth-century classic *Tale of Genji*. The central container of hollowed citron holds bright salmon roe marinated in secondary stock and soy

sauce. Surrounding it are, in clockwise order, simmered shrimp, tender steamed abalone, squid spread with egg yolk, and nuggets of *kamaboko* fish paste and shiitake mushroom topped with gold foil. On the lower right are medallions of sea bream wrapped in kelp and trimmed with tiny bright squares of cucumber, carrot, and Chinese yam. The wrapping, called *oboro kombu*, is made from kelp that's been soaked in vinegar, then shaved. Each medallion offers five distinct textural sensations.

Yuan-Style Grilled Butterfish   PAGE 107

SERVING VESSEL: Square handled dish, Oribe ware, seventeenth century

Butterfish is marinated in a mixture of soy sauce, sweet *mirin* flavoring, sake, and citron slices before grilling. The slight tang of citron is a great foil for the umami of butterfish. This method of preparing fish is named for its inventor, the tea master Yuan, who lived in Katada in the ancient province of Omi (today's Shiga Prefecture).

Kaiseki Hassun   PAGE 108

SERVING VESSEL: Tray with poems, ca. 1910
ARTIST: Rokubei Kiyomizu V

A classic presentation of the *hassun* course. For the item from the sea, a house specialty: *karasumi* or botargo (salt-cured mullet roe), a food whose concentrated flavor improves the taste of fine sake, cup after cup. Steamed water chestnuts with a light and delicate flavor, grilled on one side to a golden brown, represent the item from the land.

*Sashimi Appetizer
in Unmatched Dishes* PAGES 110–111

SERVING VESSELS (clockwise from upper left): Square dish with underglaze grass design, Karatsu ware, seventeenth century; double-rectangle dish, Karatsu ware, *chosen*-type, seventeenth century; dish with flower-raft design, Oribe ware, seventeenth century; rounded square dish, Shino ware, sixteenth century; green glazed Raku dish in the shape of a cracked Japanese pepper, seventeenth century, by Raku Donyu, third-generation potter

The main ingredient in these specially selected antique appetizer dishes is *guji*, or tilefish. The fish is first sandwiched between lightly salted strips of kelp to infuse it with the natural umami of the seaweed, then sliced fairly thinly. To make the most of the beautiful flavor of tilefish, the sole accompaniment is a bit of grated wasabi and *nori*. Note the presentation in five different types of ceramic ware.

*Matsutake Mushrooms Grilled
at the Table* PAGE 112

At Kitcho, grilling *matsutake* mushrooms right at the guest's table makes for an unparalleled mid-fall treat. The cap is laid stem-side down on the grill, the split stem skin-side down, and both are covered with handmade Japanese paper that is generously sprayed with a fine water mist. After about two minutes the cap is turned over and the stem laid on top. Again, the mushroom is covered with the special paper and misted. As the paper dries out, it will be periodically misted again. The mushrooms are done in about six minutes. The cap will be juicy with *matsutake* extract,

a sign of freshness; older *matsutake* produce no extract. For its aroma, sweetness, and crunchy yet resilient texture, the *matsutake* is truly the king of mushrooms.

*Pike Conger and
Matsutake Mushroom Bowl* PAGE 115

SERVING VESSEL: Lacquer bowl with gold-leaf decoration (*maki-e*) of moonflower (*yugao*) and vine motif, ca. 1970

Close your eyes, focus your senses, and enjoy this soup combining the refined goodness of the last of the pike conger, a summer item, with the exquisite fragrance of *matsutake* mushrooms at their peak. Kunio likes to say that soup dishes are one of the glories of Japanese cuisine, and this soup, combining two seasonal wonders, is a crowning glory. Other ingredients include thinly sliced green beans, green citron zest, and pickled-apricot paste (*bainiku*).

Whole Grilled Tilefish with Matsutake PAGE 116

SERVING VESSEL: Green Raku ware plate, ca. 1910
ARTIST: Raku Konyu, twelfth-generation potter

After scaling, the tilefish is sliced open and marinated in salt before being oven-baked. The *matsutake* mushroom slices are simmered in lightly seasoned primary stock, then placed in the center of the fish and covered with a clear sauce thickened with kudzu flour. For garnish, the mushrooms are heaped with scales fried to a crisp golden brown like tiny rice crackers.

Mushroom Rice PAGE 116

SERVING VESSEL: Black earthenware pot, ca. 2000
ARTIST: Masatake Fukumori

When the lid comes off, releasing a delicious earthy aroma, one feels transported to a grove full of mushrooms off in the hills somewhere. A bed of cooked rice is topped

with a lavish abundance of mushrooms in every shape and size—Daikoku *shimeji* mushrooms, *nameko* mushrooms, oyster mushrooms, and more—each variety prepared separately in the way best guaranteed to bring out its unique flavor, whether by stir-frying in rice bran oil or simmering. The key is adding the mushrooms just before the rice is fully cooked and ready to eat. The *dashi* stock used in the preparation is flavored mainly with soy sauce; keeping it simple allows the mushroom flavors to retain their complexity and vitality.

*Crab-Vegetable Mix
in Japanese Pumpkin* PAGE 117

SERVING VESSEL: Square stoneware platter, Shigaraki ware, ca. 1975
ARTIST: Sadamitsu Sugimoto

This steamed dish is served inside a cooked Japanese pumpkin (*kabocha*). It contains blue swimmer crab meat mixed with cubes of finely diced tofu, shiitake mushroom, and pumpkin, as well as strips of julienned carrot and burdock root. These have been sautéed in rice bran oil and braised in *dashi* stock, then seasoned and thickened with kudzu flour. The pumpkin is prepared by coating it in rice bran oil, sprinkling it with salt, and steaming. It is then steamed again with the crab-vegetable mix inside. Bright green mustard leaves are scattered on top for garnish. The vine-ripened pumpkin, which has a nutty sweetness, is so tender and delicious that even the skin can be enjoyed.

Six Fall Desserts PAGE 118

SERVING VESSEL: Palette plate, replica of a piece by Rosanjin Kitaoji, ca. 1968

The original partitioned plate, by the great twentieth-century potter Rosanjin Kitaoji, imitates the compartments of a palette used for Japanese-style painting. The dish is ideal

for offering a taste of a half-dozen desserts. From the upper left in clockwise order: fig ice cream, steamed chestnut bun, flower-shaped sweetened white bean dough (*nerikiri*), strawberries with jam, chestnut roll cake, and kudzu dumpling flavored with brown sugar.

WINTER CUISINE

December, January, February

SIGNATURE INGREDIENTS FOR WINTER

SEAFOOD
Pacific snow crab, blowfish, yellowtail, monkfish liver, oyster

VEGETABLES
Chinese cabbage, arrowhead (*kuwai*), black beans, shrimp taro, Kyoto carrot, water dropwort (*seri*), butterbur buds (*fukinoto*), *sampokan* lemon

Ultimate Toro Sushi PAGE 127

One of the conditions for ultimate *nigiri-zushi*, or hand-pressed sushi, is that plenty of air must be left between the separate grains of cooked rice. In order to achieve this, Kunio's idea was not to press the rice at all, but rather to set it grain by grain on the tines of a fork. The *toro*—belly flesh of tuna—consists of an ordinary portion sliced horizontally into thirds and then layered so that it clings smoothly to the contours of

the rice. The soy sauce served with this one-of-a-kind sushi is blended soy-*dashi* dipping sauce.

Winter Hassun Course with Nandina Berries PAGES 128–129

VESSELS AND ARTISTS: Lacquer serving tray by Shogoro Konishi, ca. 1970; blue ceramic sparrow-shaped dishes with lids by Chikushun Kawase, ca. 1970; square Shigaraki ware container (for floral arrangement) by Sadamitsu Sugimoto, ca. 1990; ceramic house-shaped vessel with vine motif by Hanshichi Shirai, ca. 1950

A colorful *hassun* course for midwinter, festooned with leaves and bright red nandina berries. Hollowed shells of green *kabosu*, a sharp, lemony citrus fruit, contain persimmon with a sesame dressing, and mushrooms in a mildly spicy chili citrus flavoring (page 172). The small yellow bulbs in the center are boiled arrowhead, a seasonal delicacy. The other foods are simmered shrimp and salt-grilled sea bream wrapped in *nori* seaweed. The house-shaped vessel contains beef broiled with *tare*, a sweet, soy-sauce based sauce; the blue sparrow-shaped vessels, tilefish dressed with Tosa vinegar gelée.

Crab and Butterbur Buds Simmered in White Miso PAGE 131

A Pacific snow-crab shell is filled with white miso mixed with secondary stock, crab meat and innards, and quick-fried butterbur buds, all served piping hot. The slight bitterness of the buds provides the perfect counterpoint to the sweetness of the miso and crab. Happiness in a "bowl."

Pacific Snow Crab Hot Pot PAGE 133

SERVING VESSEL: Pure silver pot designed by Kunio Tokuoka, 2005

The stock for this hot pot was made by boiling the crab shell in kelp stock. The only ingredients are leg crabmeat and Chinese cabbage, a simple combination of ingredients from sea and land replete with purity and goodness. This hot pot must not be allowed to boil; when the crabmeat turns creamy white, it's ready to eat.

Crab and Grilled Tofu Soup PAGE 135

SERVING VESSEL: Large, lidded lacquer bowl with gold-leaf decoration, ca. 1970

Atop a block of grilled tofu is crabmeat formed in a square shape and meat removed intact from the crab's legs, steamed to just the right temperature. The final touch is provided by bright cubes of carrot and citron and boiled, minced water dropwort (*seri*), all lightly seasoned before cooking. The seasoned primary stock contains crab innards (*kani miso*) and meat. With its marvelous crab flavor and bright colors, this soup is a special winter treat to soothe the soul.

Translucent Blowfish Sashimi PAGES 138–139

SERVING VESSELS: Nabeshima ware platters

The representative sashimi of wintertime, cut thinly to the point of translucence so that the underlying design of the platter shows through. With its pleasant texture, distinctive flavor, and lingering sweetness, blowfish sashimi truly makes a feast for the eyes and palate alike. Here too, Kunio's constant pursuit of optimum flavor comes into play. The center of each platter is piled with wasabi and lightly seared blowfish skin. Most restaurants in Japan serve the skin blanched to soften it, but Kunio brings out even more flavor and texture by grilling it instead. The dipping sauce is the chili citrus flavoring or blended soy-*dashi* sauce. The sauce is lightened so as not to overwhelm the flavor of the thinly sliced blowfish.

Battledore Hassun
PAGE 140

SERVING VESSELS: Wooden tray in shape of battledore-game paddle; fan-shaped blue-and-white porcelain dish; large red lidded bowl; small gold lidded bowl

This *hassun* course brims with the special joy of New Year's. The full, delicious flavor of handmade botargo, or salt-cured mullet roe; simmered shrimp; boiled arrow-head; salt-grilled sea bream wrapped in *nori* seaweed; and in the clear transparent wrapping, black beans in gelatin. The lidded containers have an auspicious spiral motif. The larger one contains traditional New Year's delicacies of herring roe (*kazunoko*), salt-water eel, and dried anchovies caramelized with soy and sugar (*gomame*), the smaller one fermented sea cucumber innards (*konowata*).

Yellowtail Teriyaki with Egg-and-Yam Sauce
PAGE 141

SERVING VESSEL: Square porcelain dish with red and green enamel, ca. 1910
ARTIST: Eiraku Myozen

Yellowtail is at its best in winter, when it becomes fatty and richly flavorful. Here it is basted with soy sauce enriched with *mirin* while grilling for extra flavor and luster. It is served alongside a delicate sauce made from grated *tsukune-imo* (a kind of Chinese yam), mixed with egg yolk and primary stock. The dark green garnish, carrot shoot, has a sharp tang—like a combination of water pepper (*tade*), mustard leaf, and chives.

New Year Appetizer Tray
PAGE 142

SERVING VESSEL: Ox-shaped lidded container, made exclusively for Kitcho, 2008
ARTIST: Rakunyu Yoshimura

An appetizer course that celebrates the joy and auspiciousness of New Year's morning. The gold sake cup contains grilled pheasant; the ox-shaped incense container, dried anchovies caramelized with soy and sugar (*gomame*), herring roe (*kazunoko*), and salt-cured mullet roe (*karasumi*) with daikon radish in gold foil.

Kasujiru
PAGE 144

SERVING VESSEL: Lacquer soup bowl, ca. 1970

Kasujiru, a thick, spirituous soup made from sake lees, is a traditional home-cooked dish in Kansai. One sip is enough to take off the chill of winter. At Kitcho, it is made with the lees of their signature premium *daiginjo* sake mixed with rich chicken stock, so the flavor is unlike anything else. Other ingredients included grilled chicken; uniformly cut lengths of daikon radish, carrot, and shiitake mushroom; shrimp taro (*ebi-imo*); and in the center, a heap of finely minced citron.

Sirloin Sashimi Seasoned with Kelp
PAGE 145

SERVING VESSEL: White porcelain platter

Unlike a similar technique for preparing white-fleshed fish, here the beef is not wrapped in kelp, as this would leach away its brilliant red color. The meat is instead lightly salted

and brushed with a heavy kelp stock, which deepens the flavor in the same way. The beef slices are accompanied by mashed potato, Japanese mustard (*wagarashi*), chili pepper, and chives. A handful of crisped rice adds the final touch for a contrasting texture.

Flower Petal Rice Dumpling Bowl
PAGE 147

SERVING VESSEL: Lacquer soup bowl with crane motif, ca. 1970

Flower-petal rice dumpling is a Japanese confection commonly served at the first formal tea ceremony of the year. For this New Year's soup, a thin layer of *mochi*, or glutinous rice dough, encases a shrimp paste filling called *ebi-shinjo*, a length of dark burdock root, and red Kyoto carrot; the dumpling is covered with diamond-shaped pieces of daikon radish and gold foil, secured with spinach, and topped with a knot of bitter orange zest. The broth is primary stock. This elegant soup creates a celebratory mood for the start of the new year.

Low-Temperature Sukiyaki
PAGE 148

SERVING VESSEL: Lidded bowl with daffodil motif, ca. 1970

The stock is Kunio's trademark sauce, made by first simmering red wine, brandy, chicken stock, and other ingredients until they thicken, and then blending them (see also page 180). In place of the beaten raw egg normally used for sukiyaki, he uses an orange-colored custard sauce made with egg yolk and the chicken stock. The effect is a European-style sukiyaki. The trick here is to heat the sauce to just the right temperature to maintain the optimum flavor of the beef. After extensive experimenting, Kunio has determined this to be precisely 150°F (65°C). At this magical temperature, the meat comes out to perfection. The other ingredients are grilled turnip, long onion, and Japanese pumpkin. Garnished with truffles and arugula.

Eggs Kunio   PAGE 149

SERVING VESSEL: Green Raku ware bowl, ca. 1975
ARTIST: Kahei Shima

The ingredients are lightly boiled eggs with liquid whites ("hot-spring eggs," or *onsen tamago*; see the Food Notes for *Cold Summer Noodles Set in Bamboo* on page 179), and roast beef and shiitake mushrooms, charcoal-grilled separately and finely minced. The dish is garnished with garlic chips and perilla blossoms. The sauce is the one used in the previous dish, *Low-Temperature Sukiyaki*. Mix it up, take a bite, and experience a revelation. In a single dish, the diner can witness the full spectrum of Kunio's culinary world.

Spicy Blowfish Horaku-yaki   PAGE 153

In connection with the *setsubun* festival, which takes place early in February, this dish uses unglazed clay plates called *horaku* for both cooking and serving. Wrapped up and hidden inside the vessels are sizable chunks of bone-in blowfish, marinated in a mixture of soy sauce, *mirin*, sake, and sugar, and grilled. A piece of grilled shiitake mushroom is also included. The final touch is a dash of ground chili pepper (*ichimi*).

Devil's Tongue Pasta   PAGE 154

SERVING VESSEL: Square white porcelain dish by Richard Ginori

Perhaps the ultimate in extravagant and luscious diet fare, this mouth-watering dish is made not with actual pasta but with opaque threads of devil's tongue root (*ito konnyaku*),

a traditional food that has almost no calories. It is served with boiled and sautéed monkfish liver (*anko no kimo*) and morsels of seared blowfish. The sauce is also made using monkfish liver. Pistachio halves, tender *kinome* (prickly ash) leaves, and bits of gold foil provide color accents. The character for "good wishes" inscribed on the plate using *moromi* soy sauce is brushed by Kunio himself.

Shark Fin Rice Bowl   PAGE 154

SERVING VESSEL: Red Raku ware, ca. 1935
ARTIST: Kahei Shima

The name of this dish suggests a rare gourmet treat, and that is exactly what it is. The shark fin is first simmered in deeply flavored chicken stock made with plenty of bone marrow. Pungent chicken soup (see *Clear Chicken Kelp Soup*, page 174) is combined with kudzu flour to make a thick, soy-tinged *an* sauce. On top is a fistful of light crisped rice, along with green onion and a sprinkling of powdered red pepper and ground prickly ash pods to bind it all together. Savory grilled long onions complete the picture. Not a dish to be poked at genteelly, but to be devoured with gusto.

Oyster Rice   PAGE 155

SERVING VESSEL: Black earthenware pot, ca. 2000
ARTIST: Masatake Fukumori

The lid of the pot comes off to release the irresistible aroma of oysters mingled with a subtle hint of soy sauce. Some of the oysters are deep-fried; others are simmered briefly in kelp stock, which is then used to make the rice. Just as the heat is turned off, both kinds of oysters are arranged on the rice

and chopped water dropwort (*seri*) is scattered on top. Kunio has removed the black edges from the oyster meat, as he maintains that they do not taste good—once again defying conventional thinking in pursuit of pure, perfect flavor.

Sampokan Lemon Gelatin   PAGE 156

SERVING VESSEL: White-glazed stoneware plate with calligraphy (under food), ca. 1970
ARTIST: Sadamitsu Sugimoto

Sampokan is a kind of bitter orange grown in Wakayama Prefecture. The juice is mixed with sugar and thickened with gelatin to make a refreshing and tartly flavorful dessert that doesn't weigh heavily on the stomach.

Mascarpone Dessert   PAGE 156

In appearance, these round balls are identical to the savory hot Kansai snack called *takoyaki* (fried octopus balls), but they are made with mascarpone, and drizzled with a dark sauce of boiled port wine and honey. In place of the dusting of *nori* seaweed flakes seen on *takoyaki*, they are topped with finely chopped pistachio. The sauce alongside consists of luscious whipped cream mixed with bits of persimmon marinated in vintage rum, studded with tender mint leaves. A fabulously delicious dessert created by the free exercise of imagination.

GLOSSARY

A

abura-age: Thin sheets of deep-fried tofu.

akagai (red ark clam): Also called cockle or blood clam, this shellfish is at its best in spring, when it is served sashimi-style.

amadai (tilefish): Also called red tilefish or Japanese horsehead; known as *guji* in the Kansai region. A fairly small fish with a foreshortened head, reddish-orange skin, and white flesh.

amazake: A cultured drink made from rice and *koji* spores (*Aspergillus oryzae*), which are also used to make sake. This naturally sweet drink is served hot in winter, often topped with grated ginger, and is a popular remedy for sore throats and colds.

an (bean jam): A sweet paste used in many types of Japanese sweets. The most common type is made from dark-red adzuki beans; white *shiro-an*, made from white kidney beans, is also common.

an (glaze): A generic term for any thickened sauce, usually savory. Often kudzu starch or potato starch is used as a thickener.

anago (salt-water eel): Any of several varieties of salt-water eel, usually simmered and served on sushi or deep-fried tempura-style. *Anago* are not quite as fatty as *unagi*, or freshwater eels, but they have similar sweet flesh.

angelica bud: See **taranome**.

anko (monkfish): This fearsome-looking white-fleshed fish, a type of anglerfish, is a winter delicacy. The pâté-like monkfish liver (*anko no kimo* or *ankimo*), is prepared by mixing the liver with seasonings, rolling it into a cylinder, and steaming it.

apricot vinegar: This distinctive liquid, not a true vinegar but a briny by-product of **umeboshi** production, has a piquant sourness that adds spark and interest to foods.

Ariwara no Narihira (825–80): A Japanese waka poet and aristocrat who was famous for his love affairs. He is thought to be the unnamed hero of *The Tales of Ise*, which contains many of his waka.

arrowhead: See **kuwai**.

ayu (sweetfish): A small fish found in lakes, rivers and coastal waters. Known for the sweetness of its flesh, *ayu* is best in the summer months.

B

bainiku: Puréed or sieved flesh of **umeboshi** pickled apricot.

bamboo shoot: See **takenoko**.

bean jam: See **an**.

bonito flakes: See **katsuobushi**.

botargo: See **karasumi**.

bracken: See **warabi**.

burdock: See **gobo**.

butterbur bud: See **fukinoto**.

C

chazuke: This simple dish is made by pouring hot brewed green tea or **dashi** over rice. Often salted fish, pickles, or other savory toppings are included. Usually served at the end of a meal.

Chinese yam: See **yamaimo**.

chirashi-zushi: "Scattered sushi" consists of a bed of vinegared sushi rice, sometimes mixed with simmered vegetables, over which are strewn various toppings such as blanched squid or shrimp, **sashimi**, salmon roe, and shreds of thin omelet.

citron: See *yuzu*.

D

daikon radish: This long, white, mild-fleshed variety of radish is a mainstay of Japanese cooking, in both raw and cooked form.

dashi: A kind of stock or broth with a kelp base. The most common type of *dashi* is made with **kombu** kelp and **katsuobushi** bonito flakes. Kitcho's recipes are on pages 171–172.

E

ebi-imo (shrimp taro): This root vegetable, a type of taro, has a shape and stripes that resemble a shrimp's. A specialty of the Kansai area.

engawa: *Engawa*, literally meaning "porch" in Japanese, refers to the area of ridged muscle near the fins of flatfish such as halibut, flounder, or fluke. As sashimi, the *engawa* is particularly prized for its firm texture and light, delicate flavor.

F

fukinoto (butterbur bud): Buds of the Japanese giant butterbur (*fuki*). The buds of this *sansai* wild green are a tell-tale sign of spring in Japan.

Furuta Oribe (1544–1615): A military leader, Oribe was first a retainer of warrior leader Oda Nobunaga, and then of Toyotomi Hideyoshi; he was also a valued student of tea master Sen no Rikyu. After Rikyu's death, Oribe became tea adviser to the Tokugawa family. A great tea master in his own right, Oribe became known for the signature style of ceramics known as **Oribe ware**.

Fushimi- : A prefix used to denote products from Fushimi, in the southern Kyoto region (e.g., Fushimi-togarashi, a long, green, mild pepper).

G

garland chrysanthemum: See **shungiku**.

Gion Festival: Dating back to 869, Kyoto's Gion Matsuri is one of the most famous festivals in Japan. It lasts for the entire month of July, reaching its peak with the Yamaboko-junko, a parade featuring huge, elaborately built floats, on July 17.

glutamic acid: A non-essential amino acid that is a key provider of **umami** flavor in foods, particularly in its carboxylated anions and salts known as glutamates.

gobo (burdock): This long root is a Japanese staple. It has a sweet, slightly earthy flavor and a fibrous texture.

goby: See **isaza**.

gori: A minnow-sized gray river fish related to sculpin, *gori* is a specialty of the Kanazawa region. *Gori* is becoming rare due to pollution.

H

hamaguri (Venus clam): A fairly small bivalve similar in size and shape to a chestnut (*hamaguri* actually means "beach chestnut"). At their best from winter to spring, *hamaguri* are traditionally associated with the Dolls' Festival in early March.

hamo (pike conger): A long thick-skinned fish in the eel family, considered a rare treat in hot summer weather.

hassun: A traditional course in a kaiseki meal, the *hassun* sets the seasonal theme of the meal. Consists of the most tempting offerings from the "mountain" and "sea," presented on a simple tray.

hasuimo: The edible leaf stalks of the **satoimo** or taro plant.

hijiki: One of the first sea vegetables to be used widely in the West, *hijiki* (*Sargassum fusiforme*) has a rich flavor reminiscent of the sea and is highly nutritious. It is generally sold dried; in this form it looks a bit like loose-leaf black tea.

hiyamugi: Noodles made of wheat flour, thicker than the angel-hair-like **somen** but not as thick as *udon*. Usually served cold in summer with a dipping sauce.

Hon'ami Koetsu (1558–1637): Scion of a family of sword polishers and connoisseurs, Hon'ami Koetsu was renowned for his lacquerware, ceramics, and calligraphy. As a potter, he was a leading student of **Furuta Oribe**. He had a strong influence on the development of the **Rimpa** style of painting.

horsetail shoots: See **tsukushi**.

I

ichimi: Ground dried red chili peppers, without seeds, usually fairly spicy. *Ichimi* means "one flavor"; *shichimi*, meaning "seven flavors," is a spice mix that includes seven ingredients, the main one being *ichimi*.

ikura (salmon roe): These shiny reddish-orange orbs, sometimes called "salmon caviar," are eaten after salting or marinating. They are slightly salty, slightly sweet, with a faint flavor of the sea. Called *suzuko* at Kitcho.

inosinic acid: A nucleotide monophosphate that enhances flavor in food. In combination with glutamate, inosinic acid is a key component of umami.

isaza (goby): A very small (around 2 inch/5 cm) transparent marine fish generally caught in spring, when it returns to rivers to spawn. Also called *shirouo*.

iwatake: A lichen, *Umbilicaria esculenta*, that grows on high cliff faces, collected by rappelling or abseiling. Considered a great luxury.

J

junsai (water shield leaf): A type of water lily, *Brasenia schreberi*, with dark-red flowers. The young stems and leaves, which have a unique gelatinous coating, are an iconic food of early summer.

K

kabocha: Often called Japanese pumpkin, this variety of winter squash has a thin dark-green rind and bright orange flesh. The best *kabocha* are quite sweet; the flesh is soft but far less moist than that of a Western pumpkin.

kabosu: A round lime-sized green citrus fruit with juicy yellow flesh. Related to the **yuzu** citron, but with a sharper flavor. The juice can be used in place of vinegar, particularly to make the tangy soy-based *ponzu* dipping sauce.

kamaboko: A fish cake made from white-fleshed fish. The meat is pounded to a paste, mixed with starch and flavorings, formed into logs, and steamed until firm. Kamaboko can have a white or pink exterior, and is usually white inside.

kani miso: The creamy grey-green innards of crab, considered a great delicacy.

Kansai: A general term referring to the Kobe-Osaka-Kyoto area in the western part of Honshu, Japan's main island.

kanten: Known in English as agar-agar or Japanese isinglass, this seaweed derivative is used as a thickener and coagulating agent.

Kanto: A general term referring to the greater Tokyo region of Honshu.

karasumi (botargo): Salt-cured, dried roe of the gray mullet. Similar to Italian *bottarga*.

katsuobushi: Dried, smoked, and fermented *katsuo*, or skipjack tuna (bonito). Thick shavings from a block of *katsuobushi* are used to make **dashi**; thinner shavings are used as a topping or seasoning.

katsuramuki: A technique for cutting round or cylindrical vegetables, most often **daikon** radish, into translucent paper-thin sheets.

kazunoko: Salted or dried herring roe. Essential for New Year's festivities, *kazunoko* is yellow in color and crunchy in texture, with a unique flavor.

kelp: See **kombu**.

kinako: Toasted soybean flour, often used to dust rice dumplings and other traditional sweets. *Kinako* has a slightly nutty roasted flavor.

kinome: Whole fresh leaves of the Japanese prickly ash tree (a relative of the Sichuan pepper tree). The tender leaves, most often used in spring, have a slightly lemony flavor. The seedpods are dried and ground to a gray-green powder called *sansho*, which is used to accent soups and hot noodles.

kinugasa mushrooms: Known in English as the veiled lady mushroom, this unusual fungus sprouts in bamboo groves; it has long, lacy "skirt" hanging down from the edge of its cap.

Kitaoji Rosanjin (1883–1959): A Japanese artist known for his accomplishments in pottery, calligraphy, seal engraving, cuisine, and lacquerware. A restaurateur himself, Rosanjin created distinctive ceramic pieces that are cherished by many of the best chefs in Japan.

kogomi (ostrich fern): Fiddleheads of the genus *Matteucia*, harvested wild in early spring. One of the most common *sansai*, or wild spring greens.

kombu (kelp): This sea vegetable of the genus *Laminaria* is a fundamental element of Japanese cuisine. Its high **glutamic acid** content lends a rich flavor to any dish.

konnyaku: A firm jelly made from the corm of the konjac or devil's tongue plant. The corm is ground to a flour and combined with limewater, then boiled; it solidifies as it cools. *Ito konnyaku* and *shirataki* are noodles made from *konnyaku* jelly.

konoko: Sea cucumber ovaries that are salted and layered together and sun-dried in a triangle shape. An immensely luxurious food.

konomono: A formal name for *tsukemono* (pickles).

koshiabura: Buds of the slender *Acanthopanax sciadophylloides* tree. A traditional type of wild

green (**sansai**) served to mark the arrival of spring.

kuchikiri: "Cutting the mouth," a ceremony that commemorates breaking the seal on the year's first jar of new tea in November.

kuwai (arrowhead): Also called swan potato or duck potato because of its beak-like spike, this starchy yellow bulb grows on *Sagittaria trifolia*, an aquatic plant. Peeled, boiled, and seasoned, *kuwai* is an essential New Year's ingredient.

kuzu: A starch made from the root of the kudzu plant. Used as a thickener in cooking and in making traditional confections such as *kuzu mochi*, or kudzu dumplings.

Kyo- : A prefix indicating that an item comes from the Kyoto region; for example, Kyo-yasai, traditional vegetables from Kyoto.

L

land seaweed: see **oka-hijiki**.

long onion: See **naganegi**.

M

maki-e: A lacquering technique in which gold or silver powder is sprinkled onto wet lacquer to create a decorative image. Literally means "sprinkled picture."

matcha: A bright green powder made from the finest buds of tea plants. *Matcha* is whisked with hot water into a creamy froth to make *usucha* (thin tea) or beaten with less water for the intensely flavored drink called *koicha* (thick tea).

matsutake: *Matsutake*, literally meaning "pine mushrooms," are harvested in fall. They are cherished for their earthy, spicy aroma and meaty texture.

mibuna: A Japanese leafy green in the brassica family, with long spear-shaped leaves and a mild mustard flavor.

mirin: Though often (and indeed, even in this book) defined as "sweetened cooking sake," *mirin* is actually made by mixing glutinous rice with *koji* spores and *shochu* (white liquor); the sweetness is cultivated naturally over a period of months. *Mirin* adds a mild sweetness and luster to cooked foods, and neutralizes "fishy" smells. It is an essential seasoning in Japanese cuisine.

miso: A salty fermented paste made from soybeans, salt and *koji* spores, often along with grains such as rice, barley, buckwheat, and millet.

mitate: Roughly translated as "to see with new eyes," *mitate* involves using objects for a purpose other than that for which they were originally intended. Originally a literary term, the concept of *mitate* was introduced to tea ceremony by **Sen no Rikyu**. It is used to add a sense of vitality in that milieu as well as in other arts.

mitsuba (trefoil): Japanese chervil. This three-leafed herb is used in salads, soups, and fried foods, and as a fresh garnish on other dishes.

mizuna: A mild leafy green with long, toothed leaves and a slightly peppery flavor.

mochi: Soft cakes made from pounded glutinous rice, often filled with bean jam to make dumplings. *Mochi* is a popular holiday treat, and pounding *mochi* by hand with wooden mallets is a traditional year-end activity.

mongo-ika: Common European giant cuttlefish. Prized for its fine flavor and texture.

monkfish: See **anko**.

moromi soy sauce: Naturally brewed soy sauce that has not yet been filtered.

mukago: The aerial seed (propagule) of the **yamaimo** yam. *Mukago* look like tiny brownish-green potatoes, and taste similar when roasted or boiled with salt. They are an iconic, if rustic, autumn treat.

mukozuke: The first course in a traditional kaiseki meal, typically raw fish with a vinegar or citrus dressing along with a contrasting vegetable. May also refer to the serving vessels used in this course, or to small side dishes in general.

myoga ginger: The pink-and-green flower buds of the myoga plant (*Zingiber mioga*; not true ginger, but a relative), often called ginger buds, are often used as a garnish in Japanese cuisine. Myoga buds have a milder taste than ginger root—more herbal than fiery.

N

nagaimo: See **yamaimo**.

naganegi (long onion): A type of welsh onion resembling something between a leek and a spring onion. Valued for its long white section, the *naganegi* has a mild flavor and tender flesh that becomes soft and sweet when cooked.

nagori no chaji: A tea ceremony honoring the last of the year's tea and the last warm days before the coming of winter. Takes place in October. *Nagori* describes the "lingering feeling experienced at parting."

nameko mushroom: Small orange mushrooms notable for their slippery texture.

nanohana (rape buds): These broccoli-like shoots of the rape plant *Brassica rapa* are emblematic of spring.

nanten (nandina): A handsome oriental shrub, also called "heavenly bamboo," bearing shiny red or (more rarely) ivory-white berries said to keep away misfortune. Sprays of nandina berries are a traditional New Year's decoration.

nerikiri: A traditional Japanese confection (*wagashi*) consisting of a cooked dough made of sweetened white bean paste and rice flour wrapped around a sweet filling such as bean jam, then molded into an elaborate shape such as a flower or leaf.

niboshi: Small fish, usually juvenile anchovies (*katakuchi iwashi*) boiled whole and then dried. Used in making **dashi** stock, especially for miso soup.

nigirizushi: Sushi consisting of an oblong mound of vinegared rice, shaped with the hands and seasoned with a streak of **wasabi**, with a slice of raw seafood or other sushi topping draped over.

Nonomura Ninsei: A renowned seventeenth-century potter from the Kyoto area and a contemporary of **Ogata Kenzan**. Along with Kenzan and Aoki Mokubei, Ninsei was one of the "Three Great Masters" of Kyoto ceramics.

nori: Square sheets of purplish nori—made from laver that is pounded smooth and dried on screens like handmade paper—turn bright green when roasted and have a delightful crunch.

O

Ogata Kenzan (1663–1743): Kenzan and his elder brother **Ogata Korin** were from a wealthy Kyoto merchant family. Kenzan was more famous for his pottery, though he was also a painter. He studied under master potter **Nonomura Ninsei** before establishing his own kiln.

Ogata Korin (1658–1716): A renowned painter and lacquerer in the **Rimpa** style. Korin studied under a number of masters, including **Hon'ami Koetsu**, before breaking away and establishing his own strongly impressionistic style. **Sakai Hoitsu** was largely responsible for reviving and popularizing Korin's work.

oka hijiki (land seaweed): A green leafy vegetable, *Salsola komarovii*, closely related to the Italian marsh grass *agretti* (monk's beard), in the tumbleweed family. The green resembles spears of succulent, tubular grass.

onsen tamago (hot-spring egg): An egg cooked in the shell at a very low temperature, which allows the yolk to coagulate somewhat while the white stays creamy and viscid.

Oribe ware: Ceramics in the style popularized by **Furuta Oribe**, typically characterized by their irregular shape, vivid copper green or blue glazes, and boldly painted designs in black iron underglaze usually painted on a white or beige background.

ostrich fern: See **kogomi**.

P

pike conger: See **hamo**.

plantain lily: See **urui**.

R

Raku ware: The Raku style, one of the most important ceramic styles of the Azuchi-Momoyama period (1573–1600), is said to have been inspired by **Sen no Rikyu**. Raku ware pieces are molded by hand and fired at low temperatures, most often with a black or red glaze. Raku ware bowls are often used in the tea ceremony.

rape buds: See **nanohana**.

red ark clam: see **akagai**.

Rimpa: A highly decorative style of painting and applied arts (e.g., lacquer and ceramics) first developed by **Hon'ami Koetsu** and **Tawaraya Sotatsu** in the early 1600s. The style was revived by **Ogata Korin** around the turn of the eighteenth century, and again by **Sakai Hoitsu** a century later. Rimpa paintings often depict images of nature on a gold-leaf background.

robiraki: Literally meaning "opening the hearth," *robiraki* refers to the transition from a portable brazier to the *ro*, or sunken hearth, for heating water, in early November. It marks the beginning of the year for tea devotees.

S

Sakai Hoitsu (1761–1828): A Japanese painter of the **Rimpa** school best known for reviving and popularizing the style of **Ogata Korin**. His most famous works depict flowering plants and grasses and other seasonal scenes.

salmon roe: See **ikura**.

salt-water eel: See **anago**.

sampokan: A type of sour orange, *Citrus sulcata*, grown mainly in Wakayama Prefecture. The yellow, grapefruit-sized fruit has seedy flesh that tastes like a sweet lemon.

sansai: Literally, "mountain vegetable." A general term for wild vegetables, including **tsukushi**, **kogomi**, **warabi**, **taranome**, **koshiabura**, and **fukinoto**. *Sansai* are a classic harbinger of spring.

sashimi: Raw fish sliced in such a manner as to maximize flavor and texture; often eaten dipped in soy sauce with a small amount of **wasabi** or other garnish. Also called *tsukuri*.

satoimo: A small, brown hairy root vegetable in the taro family (*Colocasia esculenta*). Slightly slippery even when cooked.

sazae (turban shellfish): A type of marine snail in the *Turbinidae* family, most often served grilled in its distinctive spiked shell. Both the muscular body and dark-green innards are eaten. In season from spring to summer.

seaweed: See **nori, kombu, hijiki**.

Sen no Rikyu (1522–91): Tea master under warlords Oda Nobunaga and **Toyotomi Hideyoshi**, Rikyu profoundly influenced the world of tea through his emphasis on the spiritual quality of the ceremony, rather than the opulence of its furnishings. His innovations and aesthetic sensibility have become essential features of the modern tea ceremony.

seri (water dropwort): A three-leafed marsh plant, similar in appearance to coriander or celery leaf, that is used as a green in soups, salads, and simmered dishes. *Seri* has a mildly aromatic taste similar to parsley or carrot.

shabu-shabu: A hot pot cooked at the table: thin slices of meat are briefly swished in simmering broth, then dipped into a sauce and eaten.

Shigaraki ware: Ceramic ware made from the clay of the Shigaraki region around Lake Biwa, east of Kyoto. Shigaraki ware is characterized by high firing temperatures and a reddish-orange coloration with melted natural ash deposits rather than prepared glazes. It is often used in the tea ceremony.

shiitake mushroom: This edible fungus (*Lentinula edodes*) is native to Asia, but is now widely cultivated throughout the northern hemisphere. Shiitake are valued for their superb flavor and meaty texture. They grow on fallen trees, and after harvesting are sold either fresh or dried.

shimeji mushroom: Small light-brown mushrooms that grow in clusters on trees in Japan. Daikoku shimeji are a rare variety.

shiso: Also known as Japanese basil, or beefsteak plant, *shiso* is an important herb in Japan. Green *shiso* leaves are used fresh, while red *shiso* is a key ingredient in certain kinds of pickles. The buds and flowers often serve as a garnish for sashimi. *Shiso* has a distinctive flavor, similar to basil only in its assertiveness.

shoin: *Shoin* means "drawing room" or "study"; a *shoin*-style room has an expanded *tokonoma* alcove and shelves that are built into the walls.

shrimp taro: See **ebi-imo**.

shungiku: The lobed deep-green leaves of the garland chrysanthemum. The tender leaves have a unique lemony tang. Called *kikuna* in the Kansai area.

somen noodles: Fine noodles made of wheat flour, usually served cold in summer.

sudachi: A small, tart relative of **yuzu** citron. Used while still green in summer and fall. A quick squeeze of *sudachi* enhances many flavors.

sukiyaki: A hot pot dish cooked at the table that features sliced beef and vegetables simmered in a sweet broth.

sweetfish: See **ayu**.

T

tade (water pepper): Piquant green leaves of a marsh plant, *Persicaria hydropiper*, most often chopped and served as a garnish on **ayu** sweetfish. The sprouts of a red variety, *benitade*, may accompany sashimi.

Takarai Kikaku (1661–1707): A haiku poet, one of the foremost disciples of famed haiku master Matsuo Basho.

takenoko (bamboo shoot): Young shoots of bamboo, appearing in late spring, eaten as a vegetable. Takenoko are generally boiled before being prepared in any number of ways.

takoyaki: A popular snack sold at roadside stalls. Chopped octopus in a thick batter is cooked in a cast-iron mold to make golden-brown balls. These are usually topped with a thick brown sauce, along with **katsuobushi** bonito flakes and mayonnaise, with shredded pickled ginger mixed in the batter or served on the side.

taranome (angelica bud): Buds of the Japanese Angelica, *Aralia elata*, a deciduous shrub. Often served with other *sansai*, or wild spring greens.

tataki: A method of preparing fish or meat by searing the outside while leaving the inside uncooked, then slicing thinly and serving with dipping sauce. Frequently used in preparing *katsuo* (skipjack tuna) or beef.

Tawaraya Sotatsu (ca. 1570–1643): Japanese artist generally regarded as the founder of the Rimpa school of painting, in collaboration with **Hon'ami Koetsu**. Sotatsu popularized the *tarashikomi* technique, in which ink, pigment, or water is applied to a color-painted surface that is still wet.

tilefish: see **amadai**.

Tokugawa Ieyasu (1543–1616): The first of the Tokugawa shoguns, who ruled over a unified Japan until the Meiji Restoration in 1868. Ieyasu succeeded **Toyotomi Hideyoshi**, coming to power after his victory in the Battle of Sekigahara in 1600.

toro: The fatty belly meat of the bluefin tuna, commonly used for **sashimi** and sushi. Toro is highly valued for its rich taste, smooth texture, and increasing rarity.

Tosa vinegar: A seasoning made by mixing rice vinegar with **dashi**, **mirin**, soy sauce, and **katsuobushi** flakes to make a deeply flavored sauce whose acidity is perfectly balanced by sweetness and umami. It may also be thickened with gelatin to make Tosa vinegar gelée.

Toyotomi Hideyoshi (1536–1598): Peasant-born Toyotomi was a vassal to Oda Nobunaga and eventually succeeded him as ruler of Japan. Toyotomi unified the political factions of Japan, bringing an end to the Sengoku ("Warring States") period and paving the way for the long era of peace that began with **Tokugawa Ieyasu**.

trefoil: See **mitsuba**.

tsukune-imo: A fist-shaped tuber in the yam family; like other types of **yamaimo**, it takes on a glutinous texture when grated.

tsukuri: Another word for **sashimi**, seafood that is carefully sliced and served raw.

tsukushi (horsetail shoots): Spore-bearing spring shoots of the *Equisetum arvense* plant, known in England as "horsetail fern." One of the iconic **sansai**, or wild greens, served in early spring.

turban shellfish: See **sazae**.

U

udo: A vegetable in the ginseng family valued for its tender spring shoots, which are reminiscent of asparagus in shape and texture, with a distinctive aromatic flavor.

umami: The elusive "fifth taste," identified by Japanese researcher Kikunae Ikeda in 1908 (Ikeda's findings led to the production of MSG as a flavoring agent). Best described as "savoriness," umami is sensed by receptor cells on the tongue in response to the presence of **glutamic acid**.

umeboshi: *Ume*, fruits in the apricot family, are harvested unripe, pickled in salt for several weeks, sun-dried, and aged to make these wrinkled pink-brown gems, which have a uniquely salty-sour flavor.

uni: Considered a special delicacy, uni is creamy yellow-orange sea-urchin roe. When eaten absolutely fresh, it has the consistency and mouthfeel of premium ice cream, with just a hint of the sea.

urui (plantain lily): Shoots of the broad-leafed *Hosta montana* plant, originally harvested wild as a **sansai** spring green, but now widely cultivated throughout Japan. Cultivated *urui* may be eaten raw; otherwise it is blanched before serving.

V

Venus clam: See **hamaguri**.

W

warabi (bracken): The fiddleheads of the bracken *Pteridium aquilinum*, eaten as **sansai**, or wild greens, in early spring. A starch derived from the roots is used as a thickening agent, as well as to make the jelly-like dessert *warabi-mochi*.

wasabi: This relative of horseradish grows only in clear, cold, mountain streams. Only fresh wasabi root, incomparable for its sweet pungency, is used in the best restaurants, where an *oroshi* sharkskin grater is used to grind the root. For home use, wasabi can also be bought in tubes as a paste or in powdered form.

water dropwort: See **seri**.

water shield leaf: See **junsai**.

Y

yamaimo (Chinese yam): A long starchy tuber in the yam family (*Dioscorea* spp.) that has a light, refreshing flavor and takes on a mucilaginous consistency when grated raw. **Nagaimo** and **tsukune-imo** are related varieties.

Yosa Buson (1716–84): An Edo-period poet and painter who is named along with Basho and Issa as one of Japan's greatest haiku poets. He was especially famous for his *haiga* (paintings accompanied by poems).

yosemuko: An appetizer course in which various dishes are served in mismatched vessels. Often part of the **nagori no chaji** (tea ceremony of lingering farewell) that takes place at the end of the tea year in October.

yuba: Sometimes called "soy milk skin," yuba is a by-product of soy milk manufacture. Eaten fresh, **sashimi**-style, the thin, slightly chewy sheets have a sweet, faintly nutty flavor with creamy overtones. *Yuba* is also used in dried or semi-dried form, and can serve as a wrapper for other foods.

Yuki Teiichi (1901–97): Creator of contemporary kaiseki haute cuisine and founder of Kitcho.

yuzu (citron): A round, thick-skinned citrus fruit with a strong, distinctive aroma. The juice is used in various citrus-based dressings and sauces; the zest is used as a garnish and to make a spicy condiment called *yuzukosho*. *Yuzu* is generally not eaten out of hand, as it is quite sour.

INDEX

PHOTOGRAPHY

All the photographs in this book were shot by Kenji Miura in a digital format using the following Nikon equipment:

CAMERAS
Nikon D3X
Nikon D3S
Nikon D3
Nikon D700

LENSES
PC-E NIKKOR 24mm f/3.5D ED
PC-E Micro NIKKOR 45mm f/2.8D ED
AF-S NIKKOR 50mm f/1.4G
AF-S Micro NIKKOR 60mm f/2.8G ED
AF Nikkor 85mm f/1.4D IF
PC-E Micro NIKKOR 85mm f/2.8D
AF-S VR Micro-Nikkor 105mm f/2.8G IF-ED
AF-S NIKKOR 300mm f/2.8G ED VR II
AF-S NIKKOR 14-24mm f/2.8G ED
AF-S NIKKOR 24-70mm f/2.8G ED
AF-S NIKKOR 70-200mm f/2.8G ED VR II

ACCESSORIES
Wireless Transmitter WT-4

SOFTWARE
Capture NX2
Camera Control Pro 2

FLASHES
Speedlight SB-600
Speedlight SB-800

PHOTO CREDITS

The artwork in this volume appears courtesy of the following:

Yuki Museum of Art, Osaka: pages 1 (fragment of decorated paper from the poetry anthology *Ise shu*, twelfth century, Important Cultural Property), 4–5 (top) & 16 (details from "Picture Scroll of the Thirty-Six Poetic Geniuses," Important Cultural Property), 36 (bowl), 45, 46–47, 82, 105, 107 (Important Cultural Property), 108–109 (paper fragments, Important Cultural Property), 110–11, 121, 150, 151.

Koraibashi Kitcho, Osaka: pages 36–37 (painting), 108 (square dish by Rokubei Kiyomizu V, 1875–1959), 114. The flower vase on page 82 was also shot here.

All remaining artwork was supplied by **Kitcho** (Kyoto Kitcho in Arashiyama).

（英文版）京都吉兆 Kitcho

2010年7月26日　第1刷発行

著　者　徳岡邦夫
撮　影　三浦健司
発行者　廣田浩二
発行所　講談社インターナショナル株式会社
　　　　〒112–8652 東京都文京区音羽 1–17–14
　　　　電話　03–3944–6493（編集部）
　　　　　　　03–3944–6492（マーケティング部・業務部）
　　　　ホームページ　www.kodansha-intl.com
印刷・製本所　大日本印刷株式会社

落丁本・乱丁本は購入書店名を明記のうえ、講談社インターナショナル業務部宛にお送りください。送料小社負担にてお取替えします。なお、この本についてのお問い合わせは、編集部宛にお願いいたします。本書の無断複写(コピー)、転載は著作権法の例外を除き、禁じられています。

定価はカバーに表示してあります。

©徳岡邦夫 2010
Printed in Japan
ISBN 978–4–7700–3122–8